650.14 FRO,A 9/96

D0534639

HOW TO MAKE USE OF A USELESS DEGREE

SISSON LIBRARY
BOX 849   303-264-2209
PAGOSA SPRINGS, CO
81147

WITHDRAWN

22556

How to Make Use of a Useless Degree

Finding Your Place in the Postmodern Economy

Andrew Frothingham

BERKLEY BOOKS, NEW YORK

HOW TO MAKE USE OF A USELESS DEGREE

A Berkley Book / published by arrangement with
the author

PRINTING HISTORY
Berkley trade paperback edition / May 1996

All rights reserved.
Copyright © 1996 by The Berkley Publishing Group.
Book design by Irving Perkins Associates.
This book may not be reproduced in whole or in part,
by mimeograph or any other means, without permission.
For information address: The Berkley Publishing Group,
200 Madison Avenue, New York, New York 10016.

The Putnam Berkley World Wide Web site address is http://www.berkley.com

ISBN: 0-425-15298-7

BERKLEY®
Berkley Books are published by The Berkley Publishing Group,
200 Madison Avenue, New York, New York 10016.
BERKLEY and the "B" design
are trademarks belonging to Berkley Publishing Corporation.

PRINTED IN THE UNITED STATES OF AMERICA
10 9 8 7 6 5 4 3 2 1

To Lynn, who . . .

. . . endured endless typing tests on outdated electric type-writers

. . . was pushed to take jobs in industries she wasn't interested in

. . . worked part-time, and

. . . worked the wrong job . . .

. . . before finding one that fit.

CONTENTS

INTRODUCTION   xv

THINKING ABOUT WORK   xvii

WELCOME TO THE REAL WORLD   xviii

WHY FINDING WORK IS HARD   xxi

WHAT YOU HAVE TO DO   xxii

Help and Health Care

1.	BILL	ELDERLY CARE	3	The Four Big Growth Areas	4
2.	PAM	CHILD CARE	5	Pink Ghettos and Glass Ceilings	6
3.	NATE	RESIDENTIAL SOCIAL WORKER	7	Aptitude Tests	8
4.	DIANE	DRUG COUNSELOR	9	Bad Resumé Words	11
5.	BOB	WORKERS' COMPENSATION ADMINISTRATOR	11	Get a Phone File	12
6.	LIZABETH	NUTRITIONIST	13	Getting Hired Is Like Dating	15
7.	BUD	EMERGENCY MEDICAL TECHNICIAN	16	Looking for Work Is a Full-Time Job	17

Hospitality

8.	NORM	COOK	21	Pursuing Your Passion	22
9.	CHIP	RECREATION MANAGER	23	Switching Majors Was Good Training	24
10.	BRAD	LOVE BOAT LIZARD	24	Underemployment	25
11.	DOUGLAS	WAITER	26	Make Yourself "New and Improved"	28
12.	SANDY	BARTENDER	28	Networking Etiquette	30
13.	MICHELLE AND ALAN	BED AND BREAKFAST	30	The Shy Job Hunter	32

Computers and Communications

14. HEATHER COMPUTER SYSTEMS
                  SALES   35   Resumés Don't Hire People   36
15. FINN   COMPUTER PROGRAMMER 36   Go for a Growing Company   37
16. KAT   COMPUTER SYSTEMS
                  ANALYST   38   Job Hunting Is a Team Sport 39
17. MATTHEW   NETWORK MANAGER   40   Tips from an Interviewer   41
18. STAN   COMPUTER CONSULTANT 43   People Hire People They Like 44

Education

19. LOLA   ADULT ED TEACHER   49   Jobs You Can't Get Right Now 50
20. MIMI   TENNIS TEACHER   50   Call Back   51
21. LARS   TUTOR   52   What to Say Instead of "I'm Not
                                              Working"   53
22. MEL   TRAINER   53   What Happened to Security?   54
23. SCOTT   TEACHER   55   Your Degree Counts   56

Crafts

24. LEN   STAINED GLASS   59   What to Say Instead of "I'm
                                              Switching Careers"   60
25. JAKE   BREWING   60   Resumé Writers   61
26. ELLEN   WINE MAKING   62   Collecting Unemployment   63
27. KATE   POTTER   64   The Nike Approach: Just Do It 65

Join Up

28.	BUTCH	ARMY	69	Make Your Own Lists	70
29.	SARAH	KIBBUTZNIK	70	Employment as Musical Chairs	71
30.	JOSS	COMMUNE MEMBER	72	West Coast Point of View	73

Research

31.	SHELLY	PRIVATE DETECTIVE	77	Customize	77
32.	GWEN	MARKET RESEARCH	78	Knowledge Workers	79
33.	BERNADETTE	PARALEGAL	80	Are You Looking for a Job or Not?	81
34.	HELEN	FREELANCE RESEARCH	82	Medical Insurance Tactics	83

Write

35.	WOODY	FREELANCE WRITER	87	Joys of Working at Home	88
36.	SY	PORNOGRAPHY	89	Hassles of Working at Home	90
37.	COBY	ADVERTISING COPYWRITER	90	Moving Target	92
38.	PEGGY	PR WRITER	93	Headhunt the Headhunters	95
39.	CHERI	JOURNALIST	95	The Clip Catch-22	96
40.	EVELYNE	TECHNICAL WRITER	97	Job Shock	98
41.	BEN	DESKTOP PUBLISHING	99	Buzzword Alert	100

Travel

42.	BILL	AIR COURIER	103	Justifications for Travel Jobs	104
43.	JUAN	ENGLISH INSTRUCTOR	105	Quit or Get Fired?	105
44.	SOPHIE	IMPORTER	106	Doing Good and Being in Business	107
45.	HEATHER	AU PAIR	108	Marrying into Money	109

46. JOEL   TOUR GUIDE   110   That's LIFO   111

47. JED   BOAT PERSON   111   Sectors and the Single Job Hunter   113

Sell, Sell, Sell

48. FRED   STOCKBROKER   117   Checking Out a Company   118

49. FERN   TRAVEL AGENT   119   Employment at Will   120

50. PAUL   INSURANCE SALESPERSON   121   Go Ahead, Brag   122

51. MONICA   MEDIA SALESPERSON   123   You Don't Start in Management   124

52. CLAUDE   PRINTER'S REP   125   Schooling Never Stops   126

53. STANLEY   TELEMARKETER   127   The Postmodern Dilemma   128

54. PHIL   SELLING REAL ESTATE   128   Being an "Independent Contractor"   130

Manage

55. SEAN   PROPERTY MANAGER   135   Catch-22   136

56. GRANT   ACCOUNT EXECUTIVE   137   Yes, Some People Do Value a Liberal Arts Background   138

57. ALYSSA   RETAIL   139   Go into the Family Business   140

58. CHARLES   MANAGEMENT CONSULTANT   141   First Day at an Office Job   142

59. P.Z.   SPECIAL EVENTS COORDINATOR   144   Job Hunting Expenses   145

Create! Perform!

60. JOLENE   ART DIRECTOR   149   Moving to Get Away from Your Parents   150

61.	BRANDO	ON-LINE SERVICE CONTENT PROVIDER	150	Content Will Rule	151
62.	HERB	PHOTOGRAPHER	152	Barbie Had Lots of Careers	152
63.	KEN	MUSICIAN	153	One Job Might Not Be Enough	154
64.	NED	ACTOR	154	Naming the Postmoderns	155
65.	JAY	LIGHTING DESIGNER	156	Moving for Work	157
66.	BILLY	GARDENER	158	"Everything Has Changed Except Our Thinking." —Albert Einstein	159

McJobs

67.	VICKI	SWITCHBOARD	163	The ADA	164
68.	CARRYL	NUDE MODELING	164	And You Think You've Had a Lot of Jobs	165
69.	ROGER	CABBIE	165	The Declining Middle	166
70.	GLEN	BIKE MESSENGER	167	Why People Won't Tell You How to Get a Job	168
71.	MIKE	GUARD	168	Scam Alert	169
72.	DICK	HOUSEPAINTER	169	The Top Ten Anti-Work Anthems	170
73.	CELESTINE	BANK TELLER	171	Forget "References Available Upon Request"	171
74.	SHIRELLE	DISPATCHER	172	Most Jobs Aren't Fun	172
75.	CHAD	BOOKSTORE CLERK	173	Moving for the Quality of Life	174
76.	BROOK	PROPERTY CARETAKER	175	The Blurred Borderline	175
77.	MARTY	CONVENIENCE STORE CLERK	176	Perspective	177
78.	LINDY	RECEPTIONIST	177	What Use Is Your Parachute?	178

Foot in the Door

79.	Sally	Receptionist	181	Ways to Make Yourself	
				Indispensable	181
80.	Max	Temp	182	About Temping	183
81.	Margaret	Intern	184	About Internships	184
82.	Mollie	Secretary	185	Comments from a Hiring	
				Executive	186
83.	Graham	Mail Room Worker	187	Don't Resent That Good Suit	188

Start a Business

84.	Bill	Caterer	191	Relocate or Create	191
85.	Vinnie	Car Detailer	192	Titles	193
86.	Alma	Cat Sitter	193	Drug Testing	194
87.	Darryl	Frozen Yogurt			
		Entrepreneur	195	The Home Office Deduction	195
88.	Chloe	Stylist	196	What to Wear	197
89.	Jackie	Personal Trainer	197	Disability Insurance	198
90.	Alex	Book Search Service	198	Comments from Another	
				Boss	199
91.	Bella	House Cleaner	199	Women Who Own Businesses	200

Do Good

92.	Bob	Fund-Raiser	203	Talk to Everyone	203
93.	Nan	Volunteer	204	Do Local Volunteer Work	205
94.	Hannah	Advocate	209	A Few Good Organizations	210
95.	Lil	Environmental Activist	213	A Few Green Organizations	213

Learn a Trade

96.	FIONA	MASSEUSE	219	The Jobless Recovery	219
97.	REMI	BOOKKEEPER	220	Temp Agencies as Employment Agencies	220
98.	BONZO	CARPENTER	221	To Tie, or Not to Tie	221
99.	GEORGE	ARCHIVIST	222	Resumé inflation	223
100.	SYLVIA	FRAMER	224	You Don't Have to Be a Leader	224

Back to School

101.	SASHA	STUDENT	227	Apply for Grants	227

AFTERWORD	228

Introduction

Congratulations! You've graduated (maybe). You made it through four (or eight or ten) years of "higher" learning. You survived several all-nighters and some occasional studying as well. You've jumped through all the flaming hoops that the collegiate bureaucracy could throw at you and you've emerged, entitled to the ticket to the show that is the rest of your life.

Now you're ready. You were always told that having a college degree was the key to getting everything else you ever wanted in your life—whether it is a life in the arts, access to the halls of political power, the ability to change the world through good works, or simply the right of every American to be a millionaire.

Forget about it. First of all, the odds are you don't have a clue as to what you want to do. Second, even if you do know, there are no guaranteed jobs, much less guaranteed career paths and lifestyles.

Since feudalism died centuries ago, the odds are you have not inherited a fixed role in society. The good news is: you don't have to be a farrier or a crofter (whatever those are) who dies at age twenty-nine because of the plague. The bad news is: you have to make some decisions.

There's more bad news, too. Despite what your high-school guidance counselor told you, a college degree isn't a magic key that will open all doors for you.

But don't get too desperate. The decision about what to do next is not as earth-shattering as it's made out to be. The way the world works now, you'll do a lot of different things in the next few decades, and your first job, non-job, or lifestyle choice isn't likely to resemble your last.

The problem is how to find out about your options. Lots of people will offer you advice, but they often want you to follow one of two courses: (1) do exactly what they did, or (2) don't make the same mistake they made. What's worse, most of the advice givers probably have priorities slightly different from yours. ("Becoming head of the yacht club admissions committee" and "providing for grandchildren" are probably pretty low on your list at this point in time.)

Of course, if someone advises you to "sow your wild oats" (Middle English for "party till you drop"), ask them if they're willing to finance this important crusade of self-discovery for a while. If yes, bite your tongue and refrain from pointing out that oats you sow are, by definition, not wild.

This book is not an exhaustive survey. It's more of a model for the kind of investigation you're going to have to conduct. Its point is that the range of job and lifestyle choices that you have before you is too diverse to be categorized and organized, and that the only way to find out about what's out there is to talk to people, and listen to how diverse their stories are.

This book was created to start you thinking about the wide variety of things you could do. Use it the way you used course catalogs in the four (five? seven? ten?) idyllic years in which you got your degree. Read it to see what interests you, but do your own research before you sign on.

You can always cook up other possibilities, just as in college you could do an independent study, cross-register at another school, take a semester abroad, or drop out. This book only reflects a few of the people we spoke to. We didn't include the drug dealer or the exotic dancer, because many people just aren't eager to try those professions. I didn't include the doctors, lawyers, and professors, because they each had more than one degree. I didn't include the professional athletes and inventors, because they have talents and attributes that few people possess. And I left out the people who are sponging off of their families or "trading their own portfolios," because few of us have those options.

For the record, the names in this book have been changed. Most of the people I spoke to were happy to give advice to a few people a week, but they didn't want to invite thousands of strangers to network with them.

In addition to starting you thinking about your options, this book is designed to help answer all those "uncles" who will criticize you for being out of work or changing jobs. Despite the tradition of honoring your elders, these guys are almost always wrong. The world has changed. And despite their good intentions, their criticism is often harmful. Job hunting involves a lot of rejection, and the last thing you need is someone who's supposed to be on your side attacking your self-esteem. You've got to be positive about yourself and your skills in order to get even the most basic jobs; no one (except perhaps a funeral director) wants to hire someone who seems gloomy and morose. That's why it's important to arm yourself against all of the inevitable comments from people whose working life happened at another time, when things were different.

If it takes you a long time to find a job, or to find the right job, it doesn't necessarily mean you're inept or lazy. You need to know the new realities, and be ready to communicate them to know-it-all uncles. The "system" right now is set up to have a certain amount of unemployment in it at all times. It's not set up to give you a lifetime job or career. Conventional wisdom is that jumping from job to job "looks bad on your resumé," but that stigma is rapidly disappearing; in fact, some employers worry about hiring someone who has only had experience at one place. You don't have to wear a hat into the office if you work at a law firm. Colleges, for the most part, have purposely set themselves up to ignore training you for the job market. And joining a union doesn't mean that you'll always have work.

You are going to have to, as one person we interviewed said, "Create your fate." That's too important a task to rush through. There is no linear path to follow, no secret technique, no fairy godmother with a wand to make it all easy.

It's going to be a long, strange trip.

Thinking About Work

The image that most people still have about of how people find a spot in the working world is "the success ladder." The myth is that you automatically find the right ladder for yourself when you leave college, perhaps with a little helpful advice from some supposedly sage elders; then you start on the bottom rung and climb up in a direct line. If you fall, a safety net catches you and you start climbing again.

It's a nice dream, but about as realistic as the tooth fairy or "Jack and the Beanstalk." First of all, there are no ladders, and if there were, you would have almost no chance of choosing the right one. As good as your professors may have been, few professors have extensive experience in the non-academic job market. You may have learned a lot in college, but you have no way of knowing what kind of work you like to do, and what you're good at doing, until you've tried a few things.

A better image for what you'll experience during your working life is a computer game where you have to go from level to level, killing opponents and gaining powers. You'll lose a few times, but you'll reboot and start the game again with new knowledge about where there are dangers. You'll get better and better and be able to play longer and longer, and just when you think you're getting bored . . . a new game, requiring new technology and new learning, will hit the market.

Welcome to the Real World

If you're new to the job market, it's time to accept *ten* hard truths:

ONE: College didn't educate you about jobs.

If you're lucky, it helped you learn how to learn. Now it's time to learn about jobs. You're going to have to do a lot of talking and a lot of research. And you'll have to do some learning by experience.

TWO: No one cares what you majored in.

Few people will even ask. Most potential employers will, however, ask if you have any "relevant experience."

THREE: No one cares what your GPA was.

People who ask you about your grade point average are probably either looking to see whether you'll lie, or just want an excuse to talk about *their* grades (or their kids'). Same thing applies to SATs.

FOUR: There's no single, correct way to find a job.

Read the "case histories" in this book. People connected into jobs in an amazing variety of ways.

FIVE: You will probably switch *jobs* every few years.

Sometimes, you'll get promoted. Other times, your company will go out of business. Even if your company is doing well, they're likely to keep changing their processes, eliminating some jobs, and creating others. And, some of the time, you will switch jobs because it'll be the best way to get something: more pay, more responsibility, a new title, an extra week of vacation, an office on a higher floor, access to the executive dining room, or a place in a department that's not headed by a lunatic.

SIX: You will probably switch *careers* several times during your working life.

To put it another way, you will switch careers at least as often as you switched majors. Not only will you switch titles or offices, you are likely to switch from one industry to another and from being an employee to being self-employed. This is merely a refection of how fast things are changing.

SEVEN: You may have to move to get a good job.

It used to be that the people you heard about who moved for work were migrant crop harvesters or people looking for jobs in factories. Now, middle managers and executives are moving around the country in search of work. Tax breaks, lower real estate costs, friendlier laws, and less expensive labor have lured a lot of companies from the northeast part of the country to the west and southwest, so a lot of job hunters will have to head in that direction, too.

There is a certain irony to this. Communications technology makes it possible for many jobs to be done remotely, so moving shouldn't be as necessary as it still is. But companies still like to have buildings, and headquarters, and employees where they can watch them.

EIGHT: It will be hard to build up enough money to retire.

Many of our parents were able to retire because of Social Security payments. And many of them were also able to build up significant wealth by staying with a company for a long time and building up equity through profit-sharing plans, retirement funds, and if they were really lucky, company stock options. On top of that, their houses, if they owned them, probably grew in value at a rate much faster than inflation. They rode the wave of a booming economy, and reaped a bonanza that put the gold into their golden years.

You, on the other hand, are facing a situation where many companies have cut back on, or eliminated, wealth-building profits. And the odds are the Social Security fund will be bankrupt by the time it's your turn to collect. (Not that we expect you to make a lot of your decisions right now on the basis of retirement, but you might as well have all the bad news, and a bit of perspective, from the start.)

NINE: You may have to have more than one job at a time to make ends meet.

More and more people are holding down more than one job. It's not that there are greedy folks out there hoarding jobs so that you can't get one, although it would be understandable if you felt that way. The problem is that a lot of jobs just don't pay enough to allow people to live the lifestyle they aspire to. On top of that, companies have discovered the bottom-line benefits of using part-time workers who don't get medical insurance.

TEN: As hard as college was, you have more dues to pay.

If you're just entering the job market, you are, in effect, a freshman (freshperson?) again. The business world has its own special social rules for you to learn and its special brand of hazing in store for you. And instead of having three years' worth of people above you, you now have thirty years of people up there.

🦉 Why Finding Work Is Hard

The short answer:

Most jobs aren't described in the encyclopedia or advertised in the paper.

The job creation and filling process is maddeningly informal and disorganized. There are incredible amounts of personal chemistry and luck involved. And the smaller companies, where a lot of jobs are being created today, often have the least organized personnel procedures and policies. If someone in a rapidly growing department in a rapidly growing small company wants you to be part of their team, the company will find a way to do it. The decision to hire is likely to be a very human one: they want you, not just anybody, because they think you'll fit in. They're busy growing and don't have time to deal with someone with whom they have personality clashes; they are likely to want you to start working and contributing right away. And the job you snag will never hit the paper.

Estimates are that fewer than a quarter of all jobs are filled through classified advertising. Some people feel that only 10 percent of the good jobs go through the papers. (Of course, the definition of a "good job" varies from person to person.

For some it's a job where you don't have to wear a tie. For others, it's a job where you have an assistant.)

Similarly, a lot of people are creating their own jobs. Setting up companies, learning trades, becoming craftspeople. None of these jobs ever hit the paper, either.

Nor is there a central, updated computer listing of all the jobs out there, or even a book published every year. That means that there is no central source of data that you can consult to find out about jobs, and no single channel through which you can apply.

Even if there were such a resource, it still wouldn't be your best shot. When you answer a job listing in the paper, you are only considered for the job that was advertised. (And sometimes jobs that are listed aren't even really available: we've heard of cases where a company has a strong candidate already picked out, but feels it must advertise for the purpose of equal opportunity procedures.) But, as our interviews showed, some jobs were created for the candidates. Employers sometimes looked at a candidate and said something to the effect of "You know, this woman could solve a problem for me; she's organized, so I'll hire her to back up my brilliant, but disorganized, star saleswoman." Or "I really like this guy. He reminds me of myself when I was young. I'm going to create a job for him and give him a break." In neither of these cases would the job ever hit the paper. There wasn't even an opening until the candidate met the employer and the chemistry set in.

What You Have to Do

Even though most jobs aren't listed in the paper, you should go through the drill of reading the want ads and responding. It's a long shot, but it worked for several people interviewed for this book. And, after all, right now, you only need it to work once.

But you need to do a lot more. Read the articles in the

paper, as well as the ads, for clues about jobs. And, most importantly, talk to everyone you know, and everyone you meet, about their jobs. Ask them how they like what they do and how they got started doing it. And don't be shy about telling them that you're looking for a job. (As long as you make it clear that you don't expect them to *give* you a job—that puts them on the spot and makes them nervous. But otherwise, most people are happy to talk about themselves and give advice.) Talking to people is the only way you're going to have a chance at the majority of jobs—the ones that aren't listed.

One person got a job when her boyfriend saw a job posting go up on a bulletin board, and took it down (not very nice, but . . .) so that she could try and lock up the job before anyone else had a chance. (She didn't wait for the mail: she faxed in her cover letter and resumé within twelve hours of the posting being put up.)

Another person interviewed for this book got his first job when he was heading for the beach one day with his girlfriend. They stopped for gas, and the next car that pulled in was owned by an old friend of his girlfriend. The girlfriend's old friend's boyfriend, who was driving the other car, happened to work in advertising, the industry the person interviewed wanted to get into. He talked about jobs with this guy, found out where he worked, and hand-delivered his resumé the next morning, wearing a business suit, not a bathing suit. Someone had quit the night before, and he got the first (and only) interview for a job that he kept—with a few promotions—for six years.

We're not saying that heading for the beach will get you a job, but this story is typical of how things work. The job never hit the open market, and his recommendation was a flimsy friend-of-a-friend-of-a-friend thing. But often that's all it takes to get a foot in the door. And this is not the most preposterous instance. Today, many people are learning about jobs and job candidates via the Internet, so people are getting jobs through people they have never even met face-to-face.

This book is meant to model the kind of initial research you should do to find out about your options, and to get you started on the process. The 101 people represented in this book are the kind of people you can talk to. Few of them could hire you, but all of them could tell you how they found their jobs, and a little about what they've learned about the working world. They aren't a "typical" or "representative" sample—there is no such thing. The world of work, and non-work options, is too complex for that. And the 101 perspectives will help you develop the attitude you'll need to persevere through the several job and career searches you're likely to face.

HELP AND HEALTH CARE

Despite all the talk about cuts in health care, it's a growing profession. Doctors may not be getting as rich as they once did, but there are still many jobs that involve people caring for other people and their health needs. These jobs call for some training, but generally wouldn't require years of school.

1 🦉 Elderly Care

Five nights a week, Bill, who lives in the midwest, is Mr. Swanson's companion. He helps him eat dinner, remember his pills, get into his pajamas, and climb into bed. Then Bill is on call for the rest of the night. If Mr. Swanson rings his bell, Bill looks in on him. If there were a medical emergency, Bill, who has no medical training, would dial for help, or drive Mr. Swanson to the hospital.

"I never knew my grandparents, and I guess maybe I'm working out a few things through this job. It's my first chance to get close to someone really old. It took us a while to work out how to work together. Mr. Swanson is so proud, so dignified. I have a beard, but he can't imagine not shaving each morning—even though he can't see well enough to shave well anymore. He shaves by feel. I think, at first, he had to keep me at a distance because of all the indignity involved with my helping him get dressed and undressed. But now he treats me like I was one of the buddies he used to hunt with, or one of the guys he went to war with.

"He gets this look in his eye when he starts talking about the past; it's like his childhood is closer to him than the stuff that's happening now. And one thing I've learned from his stories is that he didn't always have all the answers. When I started working here, I thought that he must have always known what to do and had direction because he became an officer in the Army and a big, successful businessman. Turns out that when he got out of college he spent his whole summer at the beach, until a friend of the family took him aside and told him to get a job or come to work for him as a salesman. He became a salesman and hated it.

"And, for all his success, right now, he's pretty dependent on me, a directionless kid. And he knows I won't let him down.

I suppose his children love him in their own way, but they're sure not there for him.

"This isn't a great job, but it's a job. Originally, I thought I'd hate it, but I don't. In fact, I'm taking courses at the community college in gerontology so I'll be able to get a more normal job caring for the elderly in a home. When I look at all the baby boomers who will be getting old in a few years, elderly care is a great place to be. Meanwhile, this gives me a place to stay away from home, which I desperately needed, a salary, and my days free."

How did you get the job?

"My younger brother cuts the lawn here. Mr. Swanson's son, who mails him his checks, asked him if he knew anyone who could work nights. He flew in and met me, and we set everything up: the petty cash, the charge accounts, when to call, and all that. I hate the idea that my little brother found me my job; it seems the wrong way around. But, maybe in a few years I can find him a job and even things out."

The Four Big Growth Areas

If your wise Uncle Smitty asks you why you haven't followed in his footsteps, whatever they are, tell him that these are the four areas of employment with a good chance of growing, and you're looking for a job in one of them. (If he's in one of these areas, consider asking him for a job.)

- Health
- Hospitality
- Computers
- Education

Nothing is guaranteed, but these areas are all reasonable bets. Combining these areas is also a good strategy. If you are working with computers in the health field, or if you become an expert on computer-aided education, you are likely to do pretty well.

2 🦉 Child Care

Pam likes kids; she always has. She's got two younger sisters, and has done a lot of baby-sitting, so day care seemed like a logical job choice. She's working for a day care center in a southwestern city.

"I can't believe that all these parents leave their kids with us—but they do. I thought day care was going to be just baby-sitting on a larger scale, but it's a lot more complicated. My second month here, I let a boy go home with his father. The newest teacher generally has to wait in the playground with the kids while the parents show up. It's a good arrangement: the older teachers are likely to yell at the parents who are chronically late. I got into a lot of trouble because the father wasn't allowed to take the kid—it never occurred to me. The way I grew up, mothers weren't likely to have court "orders of protection" protecting them and their kids from the fathers, and the boy had been real happy to see his dad.

"There's a lot of work involved in keeping the place clean, keeping supplies here, and getting messages to the parents. And seminars, and curriculum development, not to mention fund-raising activities."

"Baby-sitting was generally pretty relaxing. This is exhausting, both for the kids and for us. Nap time is a real important part of the curriculum. There are a lot of group dynamics among little kids, especially when you have a lot of kids with special needs.

"My first year, I was a wreck. I caught every cold a kid brought in, and I caught head lice from one of them. This year is better. I've built up some resistance, and I have enough energy to take evening classes. I'm going for elementary school teaching certification. The hours are shorter, you get the summers off, and the pay's better. People understand that schools close on holidays, but they get upset, for some reason, when the day care center closes. I'm not looking to get rich, but I would like to be able to eat meat occasionally. I also want to get out of day care before I become one of those day care teachers who talk to adults in a baby voice."

How did you get the job?

"I told a friend who had a four-year-old son, Aaron, that I envied her, and that my idea of heaven was working with kids all day. She went up to the head of the day care center and told her about our conversation. The next day, someone from the day care center came and watched me play with Aaron. That was my "interview." I was offered the job without ever applying.

Pink Ghettos and Glass Ceilings

If you're a woman, you're likely to experience some job discrimination at some point in your life, no matter what anyone says. Job areas that are traditionally associated with women, like nursing and day care, are called "pink ghettos," because the pay is, on average, lower than it is in male-dominated professions.

Also, there's still a "glass ceiling," an invisible barrier that keeps most women from rising into the upper echelons of management. More women every year are managing to crack through this barrier, but it's still there.

The good news is that, in most industries and at most companies, the playing field is fairly level in terms of entry-level opportunities for men and women. You'll still run into an occasional caveman who will growl at a woman and say that by working she's taking a job away from a man who needs to support a family. If this happens, all you have to do is discuss this comment with personnel/human relations (HR). (Lots of women work in HR, so you're likely to get a fairly sympathetic response.) Odds are, you'll get transferred to a better spot. No, they won't normally fire the caveman; they'll talk to him and put a note in his file. If enough people complain, however, and the HR folks start worrying about a discrimination suit, they might do something.

One good strategy for dealing with possible bias is to seek out a woman at a higher level within a company, or even at another company, and see if she'll be your "mentor." The odds are she's experienced at dealing with bias, and can give you good advice.

3   🦉   Residential Social Worker

Nate works in a residence for developmentally disabled adults in the northwest. He thinks of his role as part camp counselor, part guardian, part tour guide, and part policeman.

"There's no question that the fact that I'm big helped me get this job. Strength isn't called for often, but you can't let yourself get intimidated when one of the residents throws a tantrum. If you do, all hell breaks loose. If I need to, I won't hesitate to lift a resident off his feet and carry him to a quiet spot where he can calm down. We use a very effective technique here: isolate the resident, and keep addressing them by their first name. Once they snap out of things enough to respond to their name, they're generally able to get themselves under control.

"My favorite part of the job is taking residents on field trips. They really get a kick out of being outside, so we're always going shopping, to theaters, to amusement parks, and to fairs. I don't worry about the residents; I worry about the people on the outside. It's actually pretty funny to see how people's faces change when they realize they are in the middle of a transaction with someone who's developmentally disabled.

"Last year I took one of the residents, an American Indian who suffered from fetal alcohol syndrome, to a tribal meeting. It was great. It took a while for me to get approval for the trip, but I think he got something out of it. We bought him a drum and some moccasins, too—he gets tribal funds and can afford stuff like that. I can't think of anything I'd rather be doing.

"I also took a resident to a hippie fair. I thought it would be a cool idea, but I hadn't calculated on the fact that there would be some topless women dancing around and that this would be hard for my friend to deal with.

"My least favorite part of the job is the hours. We rotate the shifts around, and I have to spend a couple of nights a week here. My girlfriend hates being left alone all night, especially since we live in a somewhat scary part of town. But that's what I've got to do to keep the job.

"We do a good job here. A brother of one of the residents came by to visit recently, and he was amazed to see his brother clear his own plate after dinner. They had never thought he could do stuff like that, and so they'd never asked him to do it."

How did you get the job?

"I made friends with the Psychology Department secretary at school. She gave me the names of all the graduates from three years ago. I tracked them down through the alumni office and asked for help. One of them had this job and was just leaving it. He got big points for finding his replacement—it made him look responsible."

Aptitude Tests

If you really have no clue as to what kind of job you'd like to do, try to figure out what kind of job you'd be good at. No one says that work is fun—but most people agree that it's less frustrating when you do something that you have some aptitude for.

Unfortunately, lots of people leave college without any idea of what kind of work they'd be good at. But there are testing services that can help steer you. The best way to find one is to call the guidance office at the college you went to and ask them who they'd recommend.

How to Make Use of a Useless Degree

One person interviewed for this book found the testing services very useful. She took a day-and-a-half battery of tests at the Johnson O'Connor Research Institute in Manhattan, and was told that her strengths were in three-dimensional thinking, creativity, and design. It was suggested that she look for jobs that used those skills. She hasn't found one yet, but she knows that if she goes back to school, she'll study architecture. Meanwhile, she's looking for work in a multimedia field that would involve spatial thinking.

Another interviewee learned from these tests that his tendency to look at both sides of questions was part of what was making him so miserable in his current job as a salesperson.

One skeptic who went through the tests, however, said, "All you're going to find out from taking a ton of tests is how good you are at taking tests—and that's something most people have a line on by the time they get out of high school. It's time to stop testing and start working."

4 🦉 Drug Counselor

Diane went through two schools of learning at the same time. One was college, and the other, which she called "Recovery U.," consisted of Alcoholics Anonymous (AA) and a number of similar organizations that helped her stop drinking and drugging herself to oblivion.

When she finally completed college (this was not the four-year plan), she was determined to do something other than be a secretary, which is how she had made ends meet as she went through college. She went back to Florida, where she had grown up, and got a job as a drug counselor.

"I was looking for a gap to fill, and the biggest unmet need I knew was good drug counselling for teenagers. The resources I had as a kid were pitiful: guidance counselors whose real job was football coach and who had never had a drink, and would turn you in if you told them about drug usage, and a priest who couldn't move without all his joints cracking, and who kept staring at my chest and drooling. What made AA work for me was being around people who understood the allure of booze and drugs. I wasn't embarrassed in front of them; they had been through it all: the blackouts, the lying, the secret lives. I wanted to offer that kind of resource to kids, so they wouldn't have to go through as long a path as I went through. I wasted a lot of years. I wanted to be a counselor while I was still young enough to relate to the kids and for them to relate to me. No matter how young at heart you are, it's hard for a fifty-year-old to really do the job. Kids don't believe you remember what it's like to be horny and crazy.

"On the other hand, I have to be clear on the fact that I am no longer one of the kids. My role here is to help them, not to play with them. That was a hard realization to reach, and a hard resolution to keep. One of the habits a girl learns in an alcoholic household and in bars is to flirt a lot. I flirt without even thinking about it. But that would be a horrible thing for a counselor to do. The girls would see me as a rival, and the boys would be all confused. I'm starting to realize why some of my teachers seemed so tragically unhip. I was probably coming on to them like a freight train, and that was their only reasonable defense. I am not here for my amusement, I am here to help. Part of that is being a role model.

"It's a delicate line. I have to be cool enough for them to trust me. They have to know, without my saying it, of course, that I would never turn them in. But they also have to know that, while I understand what they're doing, I know, from hard personal experience, that it's a road to nowhere."

How did you get the job?

"I started out volunteering at the center, and got to know the administrators. Together, we wrote a proposal that got funded. In effect, I created my job. Of course, the government is busy cutting out all of these programs now, so my job may not be funded a year from now. It makes me so mad. It's so short-sighted."

Bad Resumé Words

Every job-related book has a list of good words to use on resumés: action words like *created, accomplished, led, selected, won, organized, controlled, liaison, reported, formatted, analyzed,* and, the ultimate resumé word—no resumé should be without it—*responsible.*

Those books rarely, however, warn you about the other half: the bad resumé words. Here are a few of the worst:

hung out	*lied*
flaked	*forgot*
mooched	*ignored*
survived	*lost*
endured	*hustled*
stole	*cheated*
tolerated	*fucked-up*
scammed	*liberated*
quit	*defaced*

5 🦉 Workers' Compensation Administrator

Bob works at a desk, in an office building, in an office park in Pennsylvania; his main tools are the phone, the computer, and the modem that lets his computer access other computers. Is he in the health care field? He certainly thinks so.

"This is where all those jobs you read about in health care are—in offices. I could never work in a hospital; I faint at the sight of blood. The whole health care revolution is dependent on getting files into computers so things can be managed. My job is to make sure that we never drop the ball. When a claim gets phoned, mailed, or faxed in, I have to be sure that all the information's there, and that someone is on the case.

"It's not as clerical as it sounds. The company has given

everyone on the team a lot of training. It calls for a lot more judgment than you would think. Let's say a claim comes in that looks like a back injury—I know that I should "red flag" our specialist so he can review the case. Back injuries tend to be incredibly expensive. And if it's a case that looks like it's likely to turn into a lawsuit, I refer it to the lawyers.

"What I like best is that I am part of a team with a bunch of professionals, and they all treat me as an equal. We're all responsible for seeing that the team does its best. 'Team' is a big concept here, not just how we happen to be set up. They get almost religious when they talk about what teams can accomplish, and I'm starting to agree with them.

"What I like least is the uncertainty. I'm in health care, which is the right place to be, but I'm working in the workers' compensation area. There's a distinct possibility that our workers' comp systems will get rolled in with regular health care and I'll have to join a new team and learn a new process."

How did you get the job?

"My girlfriend was temping at the company's headquarters. She got me into personnel. The rest was luck, smiling, wearing a suit, and knowing how to work a computer. They ran me through a battery of tests, but I think I would have had to have been an axe murderer to fail. Also, it turns out that I was on probation for the first three months, but no one ever told me, so I never knew."

Get a Phone File

Since a large part of your research process will be calling people, it's time to get a phone card file, a serious address book, or a program on your computer that will help you save as many names and numbers as you can. Scrawling names and numbers in pencil on old pizza boxes, scratching them into the wall with a fork, or jotting them in the margin of the book that you happen to be reading isn't enough.

How to Make Use of a Useless Degree

Hint: if you know someone about to graduate, a phone file makes a great gift.

The names and numbers you collect are valuable. Remember, you are likely to be changing jobs every three years or so. You don't want to have to start from scratch. If a fire hit our house, and we could only carry out one thing, it would be the Rolodex rotary phone file. It's the one with the big-size cards that let you staple business cards into the file, and it's full of notes about how I met people, nicknames, driving directions, and, lately, on-line addresses.

Once you have a phone file, keep it up-to-date and use it even when you're not looking for a job. Stay in touch with your contacts. If you call them up from time to time just to check in and be friendly, they'll be much more eager to talk to you and help you when you start looking for the next job. Besides, employed or not, you still want to have a social life, don't you?

While you're buying office supplies, you should also get an appointment book or calendar, if you don't already have one. Missing an interview is not a great way to impress a potential employer.

6 Nutritionist

Lizabeth is a nutritionist who works in a hospital in the West. She has a special reason for understanding the importance of nutrition: she's diabetic. She's been watching her diet and injecting herself with insulin since she was a young girl, so she has little sympathy for people who argue with her about their food choices and about the importance of eating well. She gets very serious when she talks about her job.

"We have a health crisis in this country, and I'm doing something to address it. A lot of the chronic obesity in this country is the result of personal ignorance and of institutional irresponsibility. The way I was fed at school, at camp, and even when I was in the hospital was close to criminal. We are giving kids horrible eating habits that will hurt them.

"The public is becoming more aware of the importance of nutrition, even if doctors still treat nutritionists like dogs. It's a good steady job, and I often think I do more to contribute to the long-term health of patients than doctors do. They just treat. I go out of my way to educate. It's amazing how much ignorance there is out there about nutrition.

"Down the line, I'd like to find some way to get involved in influencing public policy decisions about nutrition. Better nutrition would actually lower all sorts of costs. Students would be more attentive. Babies would be healthier. I even suspect that uniformly better nutrition would cut down on our crime problem. But politicians insist on showing off that they're 'regular guys' by eating pork rinds and stuff like that. We need to wake up.

"The big downside to being a nutritionist is that people act funny when they're eating with you. It's not like I'm going to lecture everyone I see; but if you're a friend and I spot that you are hypoglycemic or lactose-intolerant, I'll explain to you what's happening. I've even had people come over to see what I was eating in restaurants, just in case they could catch me eating something bad. They don't always get that there's nothing 'bad'; it's just a question of bad balance. But, as a diabetic, I'm used to that."

How did you get your job?

"I used the shotgun approach—applied to every possible employer in the area. Two months before I completed the last course I needed for certification, I visited every hospital, nursing home, school, and VA hospital in the area. Nothing too creative. But I went in person, so they would have a face to go with the resumé."

Getting Hired Is Like Dating

Companies seem to prefer to hire people who are already employed—just as lots of people want to take out people who are already involved with someone else. It's the "grass is greener" principle at work. You'd think that the fact that you're out of work and ready to start immediately would be an asset, but it's not. It seems that they think, "If this guy's not good enough for someone else, why is he good enough for us?"

When possible, try and find the next job before you leave the one you've got, but try not to bad-mouth your current employers too much. It's best to have a reason for leaving your current job that reflects well on both you and the company; something on the order of "I was hired on for a project and it's just been completed" often works. Just stress how much you think you can contribute at the new job, and what a great opportunity you think it is.

At the same time, whenever you start looking for a new job, you need to be prepared for the probability that word of your job search will get back to your boss. It's even been rumored that some companies run dummy ads to find out which of their employees are thinking of leaving. Having a job offer at another place is sometimes a good way to get a raise, but it's also sometimes a good way to get people mad at you. Otherwise rational employers sometimes feel very personally hurt when you leave, and go into a "how could you do this to me after all I've done for you" routine—even if they've been paying you peanuts and working you to death.

7 🦉 Emergency Medical Technician

Bud is thinking about being a doctor, and he's getting a lot of perspective on dealing with people in need and in pain by working as an emergency medical technician—an EMT—in the urban neighborhood where he grew up. He's also getting some perspective on what doctors do in emergency medical situations.

"I took a summer training course to get the job, but most of what I've learned, I've learned on the job. Emergency rooms are amazingly short-staffed, and EMTs take up a lot of the slack.

"They started me off with what they thought was a really ugly schedule—all night shifts. But I was still going to school, so it was perfect for me. It let me get to classes. Now that I've graduated, they've moved me to more day shifts.

"The longer I've stayed here, the more they've asked me to do. At first, I was a glorified janitor. But now they know there's a brain in my body, and that I won't faint at the sight of gore, so I do a lot of entrance evaluations, taking histories and stabilizing patients. One of the Ivy League doctors calls me his translator. People look at him and shut up. He's a fine diagnostician, but he doesn't know how to talk to the people here. He doesn't know what they call certain parts of the body and how they express pain. And some of the others are busy trying to con him out of pain pills.

"It's important to me that I'm doing something that's community based. For years, kids who have been able to go to college have left this neighborhood and moved to more affluent neighborhoods. I don't want to do that. I want to give something back. I'm staying. And kids can see a successful male who's not into crime."

How did you get the job?

"I took the summer course. That pretty much guaranteed the job. That and my willingness to work nights, weekends, and holidays. And the fact that I performed well and got along with the others. The guy who taught the course recommended me, and I came through. The fact that I came from the neighborhood didn't hurt, either."

Looking for Work Is a Full-Time Job

If you're really looking for work, it's going to take as much out of you as working a job. The only problem is, looking for work is a job you don't get paid for.

When you're looking for work, you should follow the same patterns you would follow if you were working. Set the alarm in the morning. Read the paper. Make calls, make notes on your calls. Go to the library so you can research the profession or the company of the next person you are going to call on. Write inquiry and follow-up letters. Use all the organizational skills you'd use at a real job: make lists, set objectives, keep records, make appointments, and follow a schedule. Keep your phone file in order. Get together with other people looking for work and compare notes.

One of the hardest parts of looking for work is having enough money to look for work. When you don't have an income, your first reaction is to cut down on your spending. But looking for work is expensive: lots of phone calls, and copying, and postage—maybe even the expense of an answering machine and a second phone line, if your roommates hog the phone or are lousy at taking messages. Plus the cost of keeping your best suit dry cleaned. And all sorts of transportation costs getting to interviews and to meeting places: bus fare, cab fare, gas money, car rentals, and, if you're looking out of town, the costs of flying to a different city.

If you have to borrow money, do it. It's not worth remaining unemployed because you couldn't afford to talk to someone.

While you're thinking of looking for work as a full-time job, remember that if you had a regular job, you would get an occasional evening or day off to relax. Give yourself a break now and then, so you can come back to the arduous task of job hunting with fresh energy.

How to Make Use of a Useless Degree

HOSPITALITY

The world keeps getting more complex, but humans haven't yet evolved into big bodyless brains. And as long as we have bodies, there will be a thriving industry based on feeding people, entertaining them, and providing them with lodging.

8 🦉 Cook

Norm's cooking for Meals-On-Wheels on the Eastern shore. It's not gourmet food. It's not even food he'd generally like to eat: no spices. But it's a job that meets his current needs.

"I was pretty happy to find a job where my grunge work results in good things for other people; but I would have taken any job—my priority was the place, not the job. I came to Cape Cod because I wanted to be close to the water in a place where people like to have fun. Now I've got a job, and a spot in a rooming house, so I'm all set for a while. I even got my first burn, which the other cooks tell me is an important mark of initiation.

"I vowed that I would never wear a uniform and I don't, although I do wear an apron and a hair net. And, of course, I get all I can eat, if I want it. The energy flow here is the exact opposite of school. At school, I was always worried about reading or a term paper. Nothing ever seemed to be done; there was always more to do. I had trouble sleeping. Now I do my job, forget about it, play and party and sleep straight through to the alarm. And days off are really days off. I can be totally irresponsible.

"Someday I'd like to try cooking in a fine restaurant. This is about quantity and efficiency, not about subtlety, creativity, or presentation. But still, there is a sort of magical chemistry about it all. By cutting, chopping, mixing, and heating, I transfer raw materials into nourishing food. And I make a lot of people happy."

How did you get the job?

"I went down to the local employment center and it was posted there. I didn't have any experience, but I was friendly and willing. And I guess I looked strong enough to lift the big pots and pans. I got here before most schools let out, which I think helped."

Pursuing Your Passion

A lot of people will tell you that the key to finding the right job is to "do what you love, and the money will follow." This is also expressed as "finding your right livelihood" or "working with passion." It's not as much of a hoax as it initially sounds.

There's a core nugget of truth: people *are* happier when they enjoy their work. But there's also an essential fallacy: for the most part, if you do exactly what you like, you'll starve.

For example, there are few jobs where you are paid to eat, sleep, and/or make love—which is what a lot of people would ideally like to do. Nor are there a lot of positions where you can get paid to go to Dead shows or watch *ER*.

But, to take an example, if you're really into eating, there is an off-chance you could become a restaurant reviewer. It's not just eating; there's a lot of writing involved, and you don't get to keep going back to your favorite places. Plus there's politics—a lot of the restaurants you review will be important advertisers and you won't be allowed to really trash them. And you'll generally have to write from a pretty middle-of-the-road sensibility—most papers and magazines don't have much use for a vegetarian reviewer (though with a good pitch you might be able to sell one on the idea). But if you had gone through the process in one of those "work can be a joy" books, you would have selected "eating" as the thing you most wanted to do and, after extensive research, found that restaurant reviewing was the best way you could get paid for eating, so you'd feel pretty good about it all.

In other words, if you can find work doing exactly what you want to do, do it. Congratulations—you are very lucky. If you can't, then find a job in which you get to do a little of what you like to do, and take that. You'll still be happier than you would be doing something that makes you miserable—and much happier than you would be if you were broke and starving.

9 🦉 Recreation Manager

Chip loves sports. He always dreamed of being a professional athlete, but his knees sustained too much damage to let him be really competitive in most sports. But he's found a way to use a lot of the skills he learned: he teaches sports and runs sports programs at a resort hotel in the Caribbean.

"Lots of people I went to school with have made it down here to visit, and they've all offered to switch jobs with me. I have a great tan, I'm in shape, and I'm living in paradise. My life is a mini-*Baywatch*: great looking people from all over the world in bathing suits, along with the fish-belly-white ocean-going tonnage tourists. And there is no cheaper or more effective date in the world than buying a bottle of wine and taking a woman for a midnight sail on a warm night with a bright moon.

"It's not a complete cakewalk. I can't yell at guests the way a coach would. And a lot of the guests are so brain dead that I have to worry about them hurting themselves and the equipment. I'm always repairing something, and I'm always counting boats and sailboards to see if someone has managed to sail out beyond the reef and get stranded. And I love the way the people who get stuck always blame the equipment.

"I am amazed at how well people treat me. I get great tips, and people are always inviting me to visit them at home. If I ever want another job, I'll have all the connections I want."

How did you get the job?

"It's a *Revenge of the Nerds* thing. I kept in touch with the kid who managed the football team at school. Everyone else made fun of him because he was a dweeb, but I always thought he was all right. He went into hotel management. He called me to brag when he got a job at a resort. I asked him to find a way for me to join him. I would have been willing to be a desk clerk. He arranged for me to come down on an expense-paid 'familiarity trip,' and I never left. Other members of the team have made it down to visit, and they treat him a lot better now."

Switching Majors Was Good Training

There's a shortage of jobs—but also a shortage of people with job skills. By acquiring some basic capabilities for finding information and presenting it, you put yourself head and shoulders above most of the competition. This sounds like a 'join the army' ad, but it's true. Even if you are not a computer genius, the odds are you are more comfortable around them than a lot of older people. And a lot of the on-the-job computers are loaded up with software that make them as easy to use as a video game. Find the information and click. Find the print command and click.

You are probably more flexible, and have more recent experience at learning, than a lot of older workers. Given the speed at which things are changing, flexibility and a willingness to learn have become key skills that companies are looking for. They want people who can catch on to new systems quickly. In other words, you could turn the fact that you switched majors five times into an advantage—it shows how flexible you are!

10 🦉 Love Boat Lizard

Brad is an aspiring actor, but acting work is hard to find. So he puts all his acting, singing, dancing, smiling and waiting experience to good use working on cruise boats that sail out of the docks on Manhattan's West Side.

"When we're out on the water, we're going day and night. The passengers are always amazed when we put on a Broadway-quality musical production. What they don't realize is that we're not a bunch of ship rats who happen to be able to sing; we're a bunch of trained performers who happen to be working on a ship. And as small as spaces are on the ship, they aren't much worse than New York apartments and theaters.

"In the movies you always see the passengers and the boat staff having affairs. That doesn't happen—although there's plenty of opportunity. The action is among the folks working the cruise. Actors and actresses. We can talk shop together. Sometimes the reason why shipboard performances are so good is that they're tapping into some very strong personal emotions. It's a real rush to play a love scene with someone you're having an affair with. You can really go to town and have a great time, and afterward, people will come up to you and tell you what a great actor you are.

"My options were to continue to work dreary day jobs and do workshop productions, or do this. The pay's steadier and better here; I do more acting, and I have as good a chance of being discovered. Plus, between cruises I really get to relax. Not to mention the fact that I am basically getting paid to travel. People pay a lot of money to go on these cruises. I get paid to go on them."

How did you get the job?

"I was recruited at a party. The people who work the ships are very particular about who works a cruise with them. You have to get along, or the cruise will be miserable. A guy met me at a party and asked me if I could sing show tunes. One medley and a little harmony later, I had the job. There was some paperwork to do, but basically, I was in."

Underemployment

When Uncle Spike rags you out for being unemployed, point out that he is *under*employed—and that given his clear intelligence, he could do more and could have risen further. You and he are on the same scale—just at different points.

Underemployment is being in a job you could do in your sleep. It's Michael Jordan playing baseball instead of football. It's a greyhound being used as a lapdog. It's an experienced executive working as a phone salesperson. A lawyer who is working as a bagboy at a Piggly Wiggly or Pathmark is underemployed. So is a person capable of thinking who is given a job where they are not supposed to think. In other words, underemployment is a college graduate being treated like a moron.

There's deliberate underemployment, where you take a basic job so you can work on other things, and there's the underemployment that results when you can't get a better job. To some extent, all jobs have an element of underemployment to them.

For the record, underemployment doesn't show up in government unemployment figures. Those statistics don't reflect the fact that a lot of people have been forced, by circumstances, to take menial jobs when they are capable of handling much more sophisticated work.

Government unemployment statistics also don't reflect people who have gotten so discouraged, they are no longer looking for work. (Then again, they don't reflect all the people who work off the books, either, so maybe it all balances out somehow.)

11   Waiter

Waiter, waitress, waitron, whatever you want to call it—Douglas is a waiter, a fine waiter, a happy waiter, at a Los Angeles restaurant, the kind of waiter who gets regulars—people who know him by name and specify, when they make a reservation, that they want to be seated in his section.

"Don't bother being a waiter unless you really like people. If you don't like people, it shows. You get bad tips and you start to hate people even more. Eventually, eventually, you

How to Make Use of a Useless Degree

'accidentally-on-purpose' drop a tray into someone's lap, or a cold drink down someone's back, and it's bad for everyone in the restaurant. I'm not saying you have to be a total pushover, but you have to be able to stand by and smile as a customer with terminal indecision goes through a few changes, or when some dork who's showing off for his date decides to send back a perfectly good meal and lecture you on how it's supposed to be prepared the way he learned at the Cordon Bleu in Paris.

"The people here are my family; the customers are my friends. I'll switch shifts to give a coworker a break, and I'll chase people out to the parking lot if they forget their doggy bag. What I can't understand are waiters who steal from a restaurant. We had someone here last year who was always making up false bills to increase his take, and who kept putting tableware in the linens that were put out for cleaning and then retrieving it and taking it home. I eat here, at the 'family meal,' because I am expected to and it helps me speak knowledgeably about the food. But I don't steal.

"Waiters who hate waiting don't last. I love it. I work nights and paint or work on my screenplay during the day when the light is good. Plus there are amazing little side benefits. I have sold paintings to customers. Needless to say, I almost never go shopping for food, and I haven't cooked for years. I am saving more than you can imagine, and will have my own restaurant/art gallery someday."

How did you get the job?

"Once you've been a waiter, all you have to do is drop by restaurants—not during a peak meal time, of course—and ask. Once you make it clear that you understand what 'front of the house' and 'stations' mean, you've a good chance of getting the next available job. I take it a step further. I keep a scrapbook of letters of recommendation from managers and from customers. I don't know of anyone else who does that, but I'm very aware of how often managers move on, and I want to keep track of my customers for when I open my own place.

"I started at a different restaurant, in the kitchen washing dishes—you don't need experience for that. The woman who's the manager here now got her first waiting job when her roommate couldn't make it. She had no experience, but she was a warm body, and the manager needed someone. That's the trick—just show up. But not at a busy time. And have your passport with you. A lot of times if you prove you're a citizen, you can start right away."

Making Yourself "New and Improved"

If you are having a tough time finding a job, consider picking up one of these simple skills that could improve your marketability. See if there are adult ed classes in your community, or barter with a friend who can help you. Learning a new skill not only makes you more marketable, it also gives you something you can be successful at, which will help you keep your spirits up despite the rejections you'll suffer when job searching.

- Learn how to use both Macintosh and IBM-compatible computers
- Learn a spreadsheet software
- Learn a presentation software
- Become fluent in a second, or even third, language
- Learn basic accounting

12   Bartender

Sandy's a talker. That's part of what makes him a good bartender. He works in a bar—not a café or salon, a real bar—in Minnesota.

"You don't have to know a thousand drinks—any idiot can learn that. What bar owners are looking for is someone who strikes them as reliable. Bartenders are in the perfect position to steal, all the cash passing back and forth. Owners don't care if you have to ask a customer or two what goes into a 'Baptist

Backslide,' but they don't want to have to worry whether the register will be there when the place is opened in the morning, and they don't like to hear about bartenders cheating drunk customers.

"At the same time, you don't want to appear too straight. That might inhibit the customers. Besides, a lot of bar owners buy booze that 'fell off of the back of the truck' and cut off the register tape at 10 P.M. so they can keep the rest of the night's revenues hidden from the IRS. You want to seem like a regular guy. And always tell them that you have few friends and never drink on the job. They're also afraid that someone will drink up all their profits or give booze away to all their friends. A good bartender gives an occasional drink away for goodwill and better tips, but not too many.

"The hours are cruel. But the action is incredible. I couldn't get a date in college, but now all sorts of women seem willing to wait until I get off. It sounds like a shallow reason for liking a job, but it works for me. You just have to learn how to slow the drinks down on a woman who's waiting. You want your dates happy, but not sloppy.

"And, remember, not all bartending happens in bars. Once you have learned how to pour the basic drinks, you can rent yourself out to private parties. On my nights off I'm on call with the best caterer in town. Part of the fun of it is that I get to see the poshest places in town. And, although you don't always get tipped for working a private party, I've gotten some $100 tips, too. On top of that, I generally get to take home all of the opened bottles. My parties are famous for my Deadly Mystery Punch."

How did you get the job?

"I messed up parking and broke a plate glass window at a bar, and had to offer to work the debt off. Just a dumb mistake. I wasn't drinking or anything; I was just watching a woman cross the street on a windy day. The owner took me up on it. I had learned the basics before someone told me that the window had been cracked for years, and was just held together by beer company stickers. I've since gotten him back, but he'll never know it."

Networking Etiquette

Since you're probably going to have to change jobs and careers a number of times during your working life, you will need to network several times. And since you never know when you're going to need your network, and it's much easier to maintain a network than it is to restart one, it makes sense to keep at least a large part of your network up and running at all times. And when your network is not specifically working on finding your next job, it can be working on finding other people jobs.

If you have ever gone out on an "informational interview," it's only reasonable for you to give them. Job networking is not a zero sum game: if you help someone, it doesn't mean there's less for you. Everyone can win. And the people whom you help now will be particularly eager to help you when you're looking. From a networking point of view, it's not best to have any of your friends unhappily out of work; you want them all in positions where they can help you.

Many companies even give their employees bonuses for referring new employees. Think about it from the company's point of view: is it better to give an employee a bonus of, say, $3,000 and improve at least one person's morale, or to pay much more—typically 15 percent of the first full year's salary—to a search firm?

13   Bed and Breakfast

Michelle and Alan run a bed and breakfast inn—a B&B—in New England.

ALAN: "We were very different from our classmates. We had an image of what we wanted: a family and a nice old house in the country. And we didn't want to wait fifteen years to get it."

MICHELLE: "Every time we drove through the countryside we sighed, because we couldn't figure out how to make the dream come true. We were both broke, and saddled with college loans."

How did you get the job?

ALAN: "One trip, we stayed at a bed and breakfast run by a couple in their forties who had bought an old house and renovated it using money they had made on Wall Street during the eighties. We expected the couple to rave about how much they liked life in the country. They didn't. They hated it. They missed the city and all its action, accents, pressure, and pleasures."

MICHELLE: "They tried to talk us out of our dream by griping about lazy, slow contractors and getting up at dawn to make muffins. The next morning at dawn, I went into the kitchen and made muffins—after cleaning a few things to get them up to my standards."

ALAN: "And they kept talking about how expensive and slow contractors were, but I knew all along that I could have done most of the stuff they were talking about by myself, or with the help of my father, who wouldn't like anything better than an excuse to come up here and break out his tools."

MICHELLE: "Plus they griped about their accountant. The idea of a bed and breakfast is that you do the work yourself, not hire a bunch of outsiders. The bookkeeping involved is really quite simple."

ALAN: "Plus they were placing these expensive ads in glossy travel magazines."

MICHELLE: "We've done just as well, just by making sure we got into every regional, state, county, and chamber of commerce listing, and by setting up a referral network with other B&Bs."

ALAN: "This is what we negotiated. We have five years to run the place. We are responsible for the insurance and all the other bills, but get to keep any money we make. (The place wasn't even breaking even under the other couple's management.) At the end of five years, we have an option to buy. We have a child on the way who needs a home. The place will never be a gold mine, but we're selling antiques and souvenirs out of the garage, too. We'll make it."

MICHELLE: "We're living a dream—not theirs, but ours."

The Shy Job Hunter

What if you're shy? This networking stuff is tailor-made for extroverts, but what if you're the type that doesn't like to gab? One answer is to think of your job search as research. Extroverts—the unshy people—talk so much because they work things out while talking. Introverts—the shy ones—are more likely to do careful research and only speak up when they know what they are talking about.

If you are an introvert, you may choose to start finding out about a company from someone other than the Human Resources (HR) folks. Find someone in the lab and ask them about their instrumentation, or in the Management Information Systems (MIS) department and ask them what kinds of networks they support, or someone in the company archives and ask them about the company's history. If you're lucky, you'll find another introvert, who will be delighted that you've asked about the one topic they're happy to talk about. You'll learn a lot, and if you decide you'd like to work there, you'll go to the HR department with a recommendation from someone who probably almost never gives recommendations.

COMPUTERS AND COMMUNICATIONS

A lot of the cuts and changes in the workplace are the result of efficiencies gained by the use of computers. If you can program, operate, repair, design, network, or install computers, you have a much better shot at a job than most people in the job market. Computers can't yet do all this—they need savvy humans to make them user-friendly and accessible.

Paradoxically, being a human peripheral to computers will mean that you're not peripheral in the job market.

14 🦉 Computer Systems Sales

Heather went to law school, became a lawyer, and hated it. Then she started selling professional software to lawyers in the San Diego area.

"My parents were horrified at first. All that money and work to become a lawyer, and then I quit. But they've gotten over it. For one, I'm still using what I learned in law school. Plus a lot of their friends' children who went to law school are out of work right now. And I still make more than my father ever did. And, I'll admit it, I did tell my mother that I could never be a mother and a lawyer at the same time, and that I had a better chance of meeting available lawyers by calling on them than I did working with them.

"More important, I'm happier. I feel human again. All law firms expect their newer associates to work insanely long hours, and be incredibly aggressive. It just didn't work for me. I wanted a life, and I like to work *with* people, not against them.

"I still don't know much about computers. But I know a lot about what lawyers do, and about how our computer systems solve their problems. I give a great demo, and lawyers, it turns out, like to buy from other lawyers. I'm still a colleague. And office managers like the fact that they can say the system was recommended by a lawyer."

How did you get the job?

"The previous software salesman, who owned part of the company, took me to lunch. It was part of his job. I griped for the whole meal. He gave me a lousy offer: almost no draw, almost all commission. I took it with only minimal changes. If I had been a mediocre salesperson, he would have made out like a bandit. I've sold three times what he expected, and I have him

---

locked into paying me a lot for the incremental units. All he saw was an unhappy woman. He lost track of the fact that he was signing a contract with a lawyer."

Resumés Don't Hire People

A resumé is a ticket—you need one to get into the game. But resumés don't give you jobs—people do. So just sending a resumé is never enough. You always need to try to figure out how to make contact with the person getting the resumé.

Write a great cover letter. Call. Get friends to call. Push for a face-to-face meeting, even if no jobs are available. And once you have an appointment for that meeting, end the call quickly and politely and save the rest of your comments for the meeting.

Once you get into that meeting, never leave empty-handed. Don't expect to get a job, but try to get useful information—and the names of people you can contact for even more information.

15 ☖ Computer Programmer

Finn is a walking example of the fact that computer programming doesn't necessarily mean sitting in a flourescently lit room, staring at a screen all day, improving some Fortune 500 company's accounts receivable file. He works in Alaska.

"After graduation, I set out for Alaska because it was the one place I knew I could make money. I had worked 'the slime line' in fish processing plants during college summers and had made reasonable money (especially since my friends and I had saved money by camping out.) But now that I had a degree, taking the heads off of, or the guts out of, huge fish didn't seem quite as attractive. Besides, the foreman had it in for what he called 'college boys,' and the conditions [were an in]vitation to injury.

"Now I'm working for an oil exploration compan[y doing] computer work. Exploration turns out to be very [data] intensive. Drilling for oil is monstrously expensive, so w[e're] doing every kind of geological analysis we can to try and ev[al]uate a site before drilling, and to follow the results of all drill[ing so we can refine our models.

"And I'm still working in one of the roughest, most exotic, rawest, most wonderful spots on earth. The hiking, camping, skiing, and fishing here are miraculous. I may crawl back to the lower forty-eight some day, but not before I have a set of photos and memories that would make most folks cry with envy. Then again, I may never leave."

How did you get the job?

"I went over to the state employment office and found that there was a posting from an oil company for a computer programmer who knew some geology. Exactly my credentials. It was an incredibly long shot—but it happened."

Go for a Growing Company

You only need one job, so why should you care whether the company you're working at is growing or shrinking? Because life is always happier in expanding companies than in contracting ones. At a shrinking company, every one of your successes will be viewed as having come at someone else's expense. Everyone will be worrying who will go next. Some may want to make you look bad, so they look better. Being on a losing team makes people mean and territorial.

But at a growing company, you can advance without stepping on anyone's toes. It's more comfortable. People are getting rich. They are happy to have you join them because there's lots to do. If you can take on more responsibility, they'll give it to you. People who got in early—"on the ground floor" as they say—at successful companies like

Microsoft have become quite wealthy while they were still young.

For the record, growing and profitable aren't the same thing. Lots of companies are extremely profitable because they are busy firing people. Ideally you want a company that is growing, profitable, expanding, and hiring.

16 🦉 Computer Systems Analyst

All of the merging and reengineering that's going on just makes more work for Kat. She's become an expert in computer systems and how companies use them. Her company is headquartered outside of Boston, Massachusetts, but she spends most of her time on the road.

"The biggest game in finance is merging companies. It always looks great on paper. Eliminate duplicate departments and save a bundle. But no two companies have the same computer systems, and they always need to bring us in there to help them merge the systems, without losing important data. And half the time it turns out that it's better to create a new system, rather than tweak up the old ones. For which we charge enormous consulting fees.

"The problem is, I'm always on the road. I have the world's largest collection of hotel shampoo bottles, and more frequent flyer points than I'll ever use. My friends, the few I have left, never know where to find me. My social life is shot. And I'm beginning to feel really at home in Hyatts and Mariotts.

"The other problem is that I'm always faking things. My company tends to take on too many projects, and we only have two real experts. A lot of what I do is gather data by interviewing people and stall until the gurus can get here or be contacted. It got really hairy recently when we ended up on a job where each of the merging institutions had their own consultants. There was someone on the other side of the table who would know enough to see when I was stalling. I called for help and a guru flew in while I flew out to take over where he had been."

How did you get the job?

"I started as a secretary at the headquarters. But since the place is shorthanded, and wanted to look bigger, they always referred to me as a consultant. Then, one day, the boss was double-scheduled and I had to fly out and take a meeting for him. I already knew all the buzzwords. I was briefed on the specific situation and what we wanted out of the meeting. I pulled it off, and I demanded that they double my salary. They didn't even blink."

Job Hunting Is a Team Sport

There's an African saying that it takes a whole village to raise a child. We should update it to "It takes a whole village to have a career." You have to stay in charge of your identity and destiny—you have to set the direction and make the choices. But the economy is so big and the job market so fragmented that you need a lot of different "agents" out there scouting it for you. That's your team. You build it by networking, and you maintain it by helping others when they need jobs. When you get a job, your team has, in effect, won a championship. Don't forget to celebrate and thank all the team members, even those who weren't instrumental in getting you the job.

17   🦉   Network Manager

Matthew got nailed by the computer revolution. His seemingly secure job, managing the materials flow in a mammoth northwest lumber operation, got eliminated. Matthew's taken a close look at the computer systems that took his job, and he knows where things are headed.

"I studied to become a LAN (local area network) manager, the guy who's in charge of how all the computers communicate with each other. It's clear that the next wave in computer implementation involves setting computers up so that they can facilitate work groups. The problem is that so many departments developed applications on stand-alone PCs, and they are reluctant to change anything. There were no real standards or standardization.

"Most people have no idea of all the adjustments I make to keep the system optimized, but they sure know where to find me when the system goes down. And they all view it from their individual perspective, not from the corporate one I have to take. To them, it's a crisis if the network gets jammed up and slows down. Realistically, this system was designed to accommodate their average use patterns, and the design assumed an occasional slowdown due to extraordinary usage. We won't upgrade until they outstrip the network on a regular basis—and then, I'm sure they'll go ballistic over the fact that we'll have to bring things down for a bit while doing the upgrade.

"Communications is an even more important field than computers, and every company is going to need a LAN manager. I use a lot of the planning and logistical skills I developed at my old job, but now, as far as I can predict, there's no way I could get eliminated."

How did you get the job?

"Luckily, there are some federal funds in this area for retraining workers. I used them to go to the community college. From there, I took an internship. It didn't turn into a job, but it gave me enough real world experience to make me marketable. A Japanese company announced plans to open a plant in this area, and I sent a resumé and letter to their U.S. headquarters telling them that I was here, had the skills, and didn't need to be relocated. Eleven months later, after a lot of odd jobs, and several interviews, I was hired."

Tips from an Interviewer

If you're looking for an all-American regular job, you are going to have to see a person like Valerie. She worked in the personnel department of a large, nationally known publishing company, and before that, she worked in the personnel department of one of the country's larger advertising agencies. Here are Valerie's tips:

- *Don't try to send a cutesy mailing.*
She's seen them all: the hats with the note that says, "I can wear a lot of hats in your company!"; the oven mitts with the resumé that says, "I'm hot"; the feather with the message "I'll tickle your fancy;" and even the shoe in the box labeled "Let me get my foot in the door." She says, "The people who send this stuff want to stand out, but they normally stand out as tasteless."

- *Get in with a referral from someone.*
This is the one trick that works every time. Unsolicited resumés, which she calls "blind resumés," just don't work with her, and she places very few ads. "We post our jobs internally, and very few of them make it to the outside. We get our people by employee referral, industry referral, association referral—you name it."

- *Call before 9 A.M.*

"If you can't get a referral, call before 9 A.M. That's when I pick up my own phone. After that, you'll never get past my secretary."

- *Position yourself.*

"It's OK to have been a liberal arts major, but you have to know how to position yourself with that degree. Don't come in to me and say 'Here I am, what do you want me to do?' I don't have time for that. Tell me what you think you could do here and why. You don't have to fit into a box, but tell me where you would fit in our framework. If you use a phrase like 'I'm interested in any entry-level position that will lead to . . . ,' at least I know where you're aiming."

- *Have some passion about the job you want.*

"Don't come in the door like the only reason you're there is that your parents are holding a gun to your head. If you are interested in an entry-level position that will lead to a job as an editor, tell me why you want to be an editor, what about it excites you."

- *Speak my language.*

"Part of what you should learn by talking to people is how people in business talk. If you talk that way, it's easier for me to envision you as an employee."

- *Whoever talks about money first, loses.*

"If you do get an interview, don't bring up money or benefits. You can talk about money if you're in your third interview, and you're talking to someone who you'll be working with. By then, we've probably decided we like you, so you can drive the process, and talk about money and benefits. But don't ask about vacation or sick days on your first interview. Concentrate on what you have to offer, not what you'll get. And try to get an idea of the salary ranges before you come in to talk to me. A surprising number of people ask for less than we'd be willing to give, and we give them what they ask for."

• *Don't make up a degree or change a degree date.*
"We check. Last week a guy lost a job because he had made up a degree. The unfortunate thing is that it wasn't a degree he needed to get the job. He would have been fine without it. But I guess he had some ego need for it."

• *Don't bring a backpack.*
"It makes you look like you still want to be a kid and aren't ready to enter the business world. Borrow a briefcase."

18   Computer Consultant

When Stan worked at a company, he discovered that everyone kept asking him about both their home and work computers. After a while, he went out on his own and started charging for the advice he had been giving for free.

"Big companies don't often need my services. But small companies and individuals know that they need to get computerized, and know that they are clueless. They hire me to tell them what they need, help them buy it, set it up, and train them. Then I remain on call to help them with upgrades and problems.

"It's not rocket science, but they're happy to pay for my services. At first I tried to talk clients through problems on the phone. It seemed the best way to do things. But then I realized that, for the most part, that's not what they want. They are terrified of losing their data or their computing ability and they want me to take care of everything. I've literally had three calls—all of which I charged for—where I got to the client and found that the problem was that the computer was unplugged—the dog had leaned on it, the cleaning lady had used the outlet for the vacuum, and all that.

"I have clients who call me in every time they need to install new software or new fonts. One guy has me come over once a week and back his hard disk onto disks. Another has me come over once a month and run virus checks, and consolidate the hard disk. And everybody and their mother wants me to give lessons. I don't charge much for the regular calls, but evenings, weekends, and emergencies cost my clients a lot.

"The thing is, I was a miserable student, and practically a complete social outcast. My eyes don't coordinate so I never had enough depth perception to hit a ball. So I stayed home and played with my computer. This really is revenge of the nerd. I am in demand; I control companies' destinies. Not that I overcharge anyone. In almost every case, I'm sure I save my clients money. It takes them a long time to pick up this stuff, so it's cheaper for them to pay me than it is for them to learn how to do it themselves. They must like me; they keep sending their friends to me."

How did you get the job?

"The company I was at was under pressure to cut headcount, and they promised me a few freelance assignments if I left. They actually paid me more in the year I left them than my salary had been. They paid me to go to trade shows and keep their demos up and working, and I charged them time and a half for the weekend days that they would previously have gotten for free. My new business program is called Mom. She tells all her friends about me. Not that I need more business."

People Hire People They Like

Salespeople have a saying that "buyers are liars." It reflects the fact that a lot of people end up buying something very different from what they said they wanted. It's the same thing with hiring: sometimes employers will waive some of the requirements if they like the candidate. There is an enormous amount of "chemistry" involved in hiring decisions.

Robin is proof of this. She talked her way into an appointment with an advertising account manager who had stated his criteria very clearly: he was looking to hire someone with at least three years of experience as an account executive, not an assistant account executive, at an advertising agency. She had never worked in an advertising agency, but she had worked in the advertising department of an industrial company, and was "pretty sure she could do the work and desperate to get the job." Then disaster struck: her train was late and she committed the supposedly unpardonable sin of being late to an interview. But, despite her lateness and her lack of the required experience, she hit it off with the executive. He didn't mind that she was late, because everyone in that advertising agency was always late; what impressed him was how well she handled her lateness, and moved on to the business at hand. That was a skill someone working for him would need. Above all, he liked Robin, and figured that the client would like her, too. He rationalized away the train problem by deciding that the fact that she lived in the suburbs was actually an asset because she could visit suburban clients by car before she came in. So, contradicting all his earlier requirements, he hired her.

An even more extreme case is Anita. She got hired as a secretary when she couldn't type. None of the three partners at the office had thought to ask her. But since she was the first person that all three of them could agree on, they kept her, and got her typing lessons.

The point here is not that you should make it a practice to go for jobs that you're not qualified for, but that personality is often one of the most important qualifications. Managers hire people who remind them of themselves when they were younger. They hire people whom they would like to drink with. They hire people who look like the right kind of person for the company. They hire people who don't threaten them; and people who listen to them and like them. (And yes, unfortunately, they sometimes hire people they find attractive and would like to have a non-business relationship with.)

If you find yourself in an interview and the interviewer is

talking about their kids, hobbies, or what they did when they were your age, it's normally a good sign. And if they're talking about something you're also excited about, don't hesitate to mention it.

EDUCATION

Many public schools may be losing budgets left and right, and as you've no doubt heard, some colleges are faced with financial crunches. But, as a category, education is growing. A big part of it goes back to the same raging forces of change that make it likely that you will change careers three times: each one of those times, you'll need some more training.

19   🦉   **Adult Ed Teacher**

Lola is an adult ed teacher. More precisely, she is a "TESOL" expert, TESOL standing for teaching English to speakers of other languages.

"I work for an organization that helps refugees and recent immigrants get settled. One of the first things they need is a working knowledge of English. That's where I come in.

"Until you try and teach English to a speaker of another language, you have no idea how complicated it really is, and how hard it is to become fluent. We don't try and turn out Shakespearean actors; we concentrate on teaching the words and phrases that a person will need to get by at an entry-level job, and to survive daily life and occasional emergencies. I base a lot of lessons on things like how to fill out a job application.

"I like the fact that my students are really motivated to learn, and that they generally come from cultures where teachers are treated with a great deal of respect. My first experience with teaching English to speakers of other languages came when I lived in France and a bank paid me to teach their executives. It was a lot less fun. But, then again, I probably wasn't as good a teacher then. I've gone to a number of TESOL conferences, and learned more about how hard English is to learn."

How did you get the job?

"When I moved back to the States, I went back to the college I started at (I left after a year and finished my schooling overseas), and used their career counseling office. There was a part-time job posting. I took it, and was full-time within a year."

Jobs You Can't Get Right Now

Here are some jobs you probably can't get in the next couple of years. If you could, you'd be less likely to be reading this book.

- Symphony conductor
- Brain surgeon
- NBA player
- NFL player
- Astronaut
- President
- College dean
- Ballerina

There are a few more. But what's astounding are all the jobs that you *can* possibly get!

20 🦉 Tennis Teacher

Mimi's teaching tennis as an assistant pro. In the winter, she teaches in Florida; in the summer, she teaches at a club in a New York suburb.

"I love tennis. Always have. But I never expected to make a career of it. I'm not that good. Turns out you don't have to be that good. I don't generally teach the hotshots. I teach the kids and the older folks and the beginners, mostly. My greatest skills are not my groundstrokes; they're patience, listening, organizing tournaments, not making conflicting reservations, and keeping the tennis shop in order.

"Plus there are just some people I'm better with than the pro. He couldn't get some of the older ladies to serve well. He kept telling them to throw their racket into the service court, just like they were throwing a ball. The problem was, none of them had been taught how to throw a ball as girls. One of the

How to Make Use of a Useless Degree

ladies told me this, and it was true. They threw from the elbow, not from the shoulder. I know about throwing: I had brothers who insisted that I be able to play catch with them. So I spent half of a group lesson teaching them how to throw balls: no rackets. They loved it. And no little girl gets through a lesson without my being sure she can throw.

"After the season, I tried to get a 'real' job. Bought a blue ladies' suit and a red power blazer, some good blouses, and real shoes; but it just didn't work for me. I didn't like being in the city, and the suburbs seemed dead after the club closed in fall. I jumped at the chance to teach in Florida during the winter.

"The setup isn't ideal. The closest thing I have to a real home is my car. Up north I get put up for free at the house of some members, and I stay in staff quarters in Florida. I'm always hanging out with people who are on vacation, while I'm always working. My social life is weak. But it's OK for now.

"I know I'm going to have to make a change at some point. I had some knee problems this year and I'm real aware that jumping from job to job puts me in danger of not having medical coverage, or having an insurance company label the knee a preexisting condition and refusing to pay for treatments."

How did you get the job?

"My coach from college set up the summer job. The pro is an alum, and he always recruits his assistants through the coach. I got the winter job from one of the ladies whom I taught how to throw. She belongs to both clubs, and when she got to Florida and found there was no one down there to coach her grandson when he came down in February, she hunted me down. No interview, no test, no nothing. Just one insistent reference."

Call Back

If you don't get a job, call back and see if you can get them into a dialogue on what you could have done better. It's great feedback, and a good opportunity to ask for a few other names you could call. Most people will genuinely feel sorry that they weren't able to hire you, and they're particularly likely to give you good names and advice at this time. Once you're hired, they can stop feeling guilty.

Ask where the person they hired came from. If they quit a job to take the one you wanted, call the place they left and see if you can get their old job.

Following up is not just an impressive example of how buttoned up and thorough you are; it's also great strategy. If the new person doesn't work out and leaves, or if another job opens up, you'll be in the top of the employer's mind, and they're likely to hire you rather than go through a whole new search.

21 🦉 Tutor

Lars works a double career. He's a tutor, who has his eye on becoming a college-level math teacher. But he is also a construction worker.

"Math is an art. It's beautiful, and I can communicate that. I hate how most math is taught. But I need more credentials before I can become an assistant professor. Meanwhile, tutoring lets me keep teaching.

"The money from the construction work lets me continue my studies. It also keeps me grounded in the real world so I don't become one of those ivory tower isolated academic types. One job exhausts me physically, and the other job exhausts me mentally—it's a good fit."

How did you get the job?

"I started out in college tutoring fellow students. It wasn't a formal thing. People in my classes who knew that I was doing well would call up and ask for help and I'd say 'Get a six-pack and I'll come over and give you a hand.' I enjoyed it, so I put up flyers and got some clients I charged actual money, not

How to Make Use of a Useless Degree

beer. The school heard about it, and instead of telling me to stop it, they offered me a job in their 'tutor trailer.' Last semester, they even had me take on a section, where students attending a lecture course got more personal attention and help with the assignments."

What to Say Instead of "I'm Not Working"

- I'm freelance.
- I'm an artist.
- I'm a writer.
- I'm a self-employed consultant.
- I've got several outstanding offers, but I'm dedicated to finding a position that offers the right challenges.
- (In Hollywood) My project is with a studio and they're thinking of optioning it.
- I'm between projects.
- (On Wall Street) I'm working on an IPO, and I can't talk about it.
- Some of my friends are starting a company, which I'll join, but they've got to wait out the end of their non-compete clauses.
- I have a business proposal with some funding sources, and I expect to be starting a company soon.

The best thing to say:
I'm working full-time on looking for work—do you have any advice or leads you can give me?

22 🦉 Trainer

Mel is a trainer. Right now, he's providing on-site software training at corporations.

"I started out as an actor, and I use a lot of what I learned there. When I'm training, I'm performing. I make a good first impression, know my stuff, stay cool, ad lib, and stay aware of my audience. And the comments which get written at the end of every session are the most positive reviews I've ever gotten.

"I had no idea this field was so big. But, from what the clients tell me, they're in training all the time. Safety training, sensitivity training—it's all like leading an acting workshop. The only thing I'm not ready to do is sales training—the guys here believe that salespeople will only respect and listen to people who have been star salespeople.

"I only get paid for the days when they're training me or I'm out training for them. But they keep me so busy, I'm making more than any salary I would get. Just no benefits. And I'm learning a lot. If I wanted a corporate job, I've certainly met enough Human Resources people—but I can't see why I'd do that."

How did you get the job?

"I took a weekend job distributing literature and collecting business cards at a corporate booth at a PC expo. A lot of actors work the trade shows—it's not just the pretty models at the car shows; it's some of the guys who look like executives. One of the people from the training company came around and asked me a lot of questions. I must have handled him well, because he offered me a job."

What Happened to Security?

If Uncle Dick wonders aloud why you don't just take a job and hang onto it so you have the kind of security he had during his career, tell him that things are harder today than they were when he started. Back then, if you wanted security, you could work for the government, join a union, or work for a blue-chip corporation. But now government employment is shrinking, joining a union is no guarantee of work, and even companies like IBM and Kodak have lost their ability or inclination to offer lifetime employment.

If you need stability, study meditation. But don't expect to get it from a company.

23   Teacher

Scott is a teacher.

"This is my third year, and it's the best yet. I've learned how to deal with the kids better, and I'm smarter about dealing with other teachers and the bureaucracy. And the kids know who I am and they don't waste so much time testing to see what I'm like.

"I love teaching, but don't let anyone tell you it's not a full-time job. I'm up earlier than most people I know, and I'm grading papers and projects and preparing lesson plans late into the night. I know there are teachers who don't do that, but I don't want to be that kind of teacher. Good teaching is creative. When you hit creative burnout, you should get out.

"Everybody talks about the low pay, but it's not that bad. I just continued living the way I had in school: beat-up car, roommates, secondhand furniture, and—don't tell the principal—clothes from the Salvation Army, Goodwill, and the school's annual tag sale. It all works out just fine. Of course, if I were to try to raise a family on this salary, it would be pretty tough.

"I could live better if I worked during summers, but I think a lot of teachers make a mistake when they don't take the summer off. You need the time to recharge, and it's the only reasonable time to take courses that will improve your skills and your pay. It's also the only time I really get away from this community. When I'm here, I have to be a good role model. When I'm away, no one calls me 'Mr.,' or cares if—or what—I smoke.

"The benefit that you don't hear about is that you really learn a lot when you're a teacher. Teaching methods have gotten better, and a lot of stuff I learned by rote, I now, finally, understand. It's like having a light suddenly turn on."

How did you get the job?

"I registered with the city as a substitute teacher. You don't need to be certified to do that; you just need to intend to get certified. I saw a lot of schools and was exposed to a lot of teaching methods. I kept taking classes toward certification. One principal decided he liked me and I started getting all their sub calls. A good principal looks in on subs, because kids really like to mess with subs and unless you've really got your act together they will hijack the class, tell you all the wrong names, and convince you that you've been handed the wrong lesson plan. When a teacher left, I had a job for the rest of the year, and for the next year."

Your Degree Counts

There is a difference between having a degree and not having one. Things may seem pretty desperate to you right now—but talk to someone without a degree and you'll find that they feel even more desperate. They've found that the first step in a lot of screening for jobs is to throw out everyone who doesn't have a degree. It's called the "paper ceiling." If you don't have a diploma, it's hard to rise above it.

Your degree counts, but your diploma doesn't. No one will ever ask to see it. So, if your mother, father, grandparents, etc. don't want it, and you're not the type to frame it and hang it up, feel free to use it to line the birdcage or laminate it and use it as a placemat.

CRAFTS

The Middle Ages may be dead, but there are still plenty of artisans from whom you can learn. It's unlikely that you'll ever get rich as a mason, stained glass maker, brewer, weaver, bookbinder, potter, or cabinetmaker, but you may find the work deeply satisfying.

Many of these crafts can be sampled through adult education classes. Call the nearest college or the local Y to see if there are classes available. Find an artisan at a local crafts fair and ask them if they teach anywhere.

If you like your first taste of a trade, talk to everyone you can find who knows about it. Check the phone book, for a start. If there's a historical recreation nearby (like Sturbridge Village in Sturbridge, Massachusetts), contact them.

Often craftspeople will take on apprentices. Apprentices sometimes work for nothing, sometimes get room and board, and occasionally get a meager salary—but their main form of payment for all the menial tasks they are asked to do is learning the trade. And if an apprentice learns a trade well, someday they can set up shop as a master craftsperson and take on an apprentice or two.

24 Stained Glass

Len is an apprentice to a stained glass artisan. He works in a loft filled with colorful sheets of glass, pieces of wood, and rolls of leading. He works on assigned projects all day. When he has the energy, he stays late, changes the radio station, and works on his own projects.

"As is traditional with apprentices, my pay is next to nothing. I do a lot of cleaning up and running to the lumber yard or the hardware store. And rather than getting formal instruction, I learn by doing, by watching, and by occasionally getting yelled at.

"But I am getting better. When I go home to my parents and see the stuff I made them a year ago (first rule of crafts apprenticeship: make all gifts), I'm embarrassed. And I think I'm lucky: I get to learn in this country; the guy I'm learning from had to go to Europe. It's not as simple a business as you think. Anyone can make cute giftos for crafts fairs. What I'm learning is the real art of windows, doors, room dividers, and skylights.

"These larger commissions bring in a lot more money, and they challenge your creativity a lot more. It's like painting a mural in glass, and it involves a lot of sketching and planning, and creating very tight specifications. I hate to admit it, but my math teachers were right: I did end up doing something where understanding fractions is essential.

"You wouldn't think it, but this is very physical work. I've grown some muscles. Glass is heavy, and so are lead and wood."

How did you get the job?

"You'd think that since I'm basically a slave, getting the job would have been easy. But there was a real process. The master craftsman wanted to be sure I was the right kind of person for his workshop. I had to ask, to write an essay on why I wanted to be an apprentice, to critique a piece, and to draw a design for a piece. If the question is how did I find the guy, the answer is fate. I was doing a photo essay on old trolley tracks, and the tracks went right by his studio. I looked in the window and was hooked. Of course it may just have been one of those lighting tricks we help people with. Half the windows we put in are designed to throw a special light on a person in a particular position."

What to Say Instead of "I'm Switching Careers"

Instead of telling people that you are giving up on a profession, tell them that you are re-careering. Re-careering sounds more purposeful. It implies that you have a plan. When you say re-careering, a lot of people will ask you to explain it. Here are some ways:

- Tell culture buffs that re-careering is like waltzing: there are some slow steps—and some backward steps—in the dance.
- Tell sports nuts it's like dropping back to throw a forward pass.
- Tell mothers it's like a baby's development: after a big leap forward, like rolling over, there's a short period of regression and consolidation before the next leap.

25 Brewing

Jake works for a microbrewery. If the image that comes to mind is an old wooden building with big oak vats and hoppers full of grain, forget it. The beer is brewed in a flourescent-lit, concrete-floored industrial space with large, gleaming steel tanks. And Jake wears jeans, not lederhosen.

"My image of the little old beer maker was of a jolly, slow moving, pot bellied guy. The boss here is thin as a rail and moves a thousand miles an hour. We stay in good shape, because we're always hauling something somewhere and moving something somewhere else.

"Until you start making beer, you have no idea of how much effort goes into making it, and how many ways it could go wrong. And there's nothing sadder than having to dump a batch that's beyond hope. That doesn't happen often: you check the beer all the time, and there are all sorts of additives you use to keep it on track. Next time you meet a brewer, ask him about fish tailings; it's not something they usually talk about.

"A big part of my job is cleaning. We're always washing things down to avoid contamination. So I could always get a job as a janitor. I'm enjoying learning about beer making, but I'm not sure I want to start my own microbrewery. It's an incredible amount of work. Even if I wanted to, I don't know if I'll ever be able to go into business for myself. There are a lot of start-up costs and most of the cities which have good enough water and sewerage already have breweries.

"The main drawback to this are that I can never speed. When you smell like a brewery, that's asking for trouble."

How did you get the job?

"I got the job because I had a truck. The boss's truck broke down; we had mutual friends. I helped him haul some barrels. I needed a job. He didn't want to buy a new truck just yet. It all worked out."

Resumé Writers

A lot of people could write a novel faster than they can write their resumé. Call them on the first day of their job search, and that's the day they're starting their resumé. Call them two weeks later, and they're still at it. They've gotten a book from the library or a bookstore that gives them the format, but they still can't get it done.

If you are absolutely hung up on getting your resumé written, get help. It's not worth losing all that time on something that just shouldn't take that long to do. Check the career office from the school you went to, and see if they'll help you, or look in the local paper for an ad from a professional.

Amanda's an example of someone who benefited from a session with a professional resumé writer. "While I don't think I kept a word she wrote on my final resumé, the process was important. The questions she asked taught me how to present my experience. I came in thinking I had no experience, but I learned I had a lot. Later, when I heard myself thinking that I was completely unqualified to do research, I rethought things and realized that a lot of what they wanted me to do in research involved secretarial skills that I had a lot of practice at."

Another hint is to stop worrying so much about the one perfect resumé and write three different ones. For some reason, that's easier and faster for a lot of people. Then choose whichever resumé is best targeted for each opportunity.

26 🦉 Wine Making

Ellen's working for a small West Coast wine maker. She does a lot of the testing and record keeping. She answers the phone. During bottling, she does some foiling and capping. The place is small.

"I'm a wine nut. I went to Europe for a while and was a 'wine slave' so I could learn something about how wine is made. Now I'm learning more about how the business works, and a lot more about the fine points of making it. (A lot of the Europeans turned out to be pretty secretive about their craft.) The hours are endless. The pay is miserable, but we're like a family—a family that really knows how to celebrate—and I'm having the time of my life.

"Plus I've gotten to take enough bottles home that I've got the basis for a valuable cellar, and I've been able to give better presents to my friends than I could ever afford. There's no school you can go to to learn this business. And you certainly can't learn it out of books. It's all color, feel, taste, and smell. This is how you do it."

How did you get the job?

"I chose three companies that made wine good enough for me to want to be associated with. Then I went and hung around the wineries to see where the chemistry was best. I told them all I wanted a job, and hung around the one I liked best and did whatever I could to make myself useful until I got hired. It's like I did two apprenticeships—one in Europe and one here. What put me over the top was when a wine critic, whose word is like the Bible to the people who buy good wine, remembered my name and asked my opinion about a vintage. The wine maker here knew he had to do something to keep me, and that something was a job."

Collecting Unemployment

The fact that you will be out of work now and again, no matter how good and diligent you are, means that it's likely that you may qualify for unemployment compensation at some point. Some people are ashamed to collect unemployment, just as some people are ashamed to collect welfare when they need it.

This seems like misplaced pride. These support systems are there for a reason. They are designed to help people through rough times.

Even if you have a problem with the idea of collecting welfare when you need it, you should not extend this logic to unemployment. Unemployment, like social security, is a payment from a system that you pay into. When you have a job, you support the unemployment compensation system with your taxes. Unemployment compensation exists to help you stay afloat until you find the next job. As long as you are seriously looking for work while you are collecting unemployment, you've got nothing to be ashamed of; you are fulfilling your part of the bargain.

Unfortunately, there are no unemployment payments for people who are looking for their first jobs. And, given the way politics are going, there may soon be next to no unemployment compensation.

27 🦉 Potter

Kate is becoming a potter. Someday she wants a farmhouse with a kiln in the barn. But that's down the road. Right now she's learning. She calls what she's doing now "centering;" it's a pottery term, but it also describes the personal process she's going through of finding who she is and what she really wants to do.

"I don't know what it is about pottery. Every part of it is mesmerizing for me. Feeling the clay in my hands, shaping it, feeling it spin. It's what I have to do.

"I tried to take pottery classes while holding down a regular job, but it was just too schizophrenic. I was always staying too late to finish a piece, always tired at work. It was like there was two of me: one in a suit, who stayed clean; and one in jeans and a T-shirt covered in clay. I wanted to be the clay one. So now I work here. I ring up sales in the front of the shop, schedule classes, collect tuition, put up flyers, and do a lot of pottery.

"My family says I should try and sell my work as art. But they're family. They've always wanted me to be an artist, particularly my father, who, at heart, doesn't really believe that females need to go to college. That's the only thing that makes me hesitant about what I've done. I don't want my father to think he was right. But living my life to spite his opinions would be as wrong for me as living my life according to his instructions. I've had to move beyond that.

"I don't know where this is taking me. It's not what you'd call a classic career move. But I am willing to justify the pay cut I took by looking at all the joy I get. Plus I save money on dry cleaning, and by not having to buy tons of aspirin and Mylanta, and I've stopped going to the shrink. I thought talking was what I needed. It wasn't. I needed something tactile— we weren't a touching family. I needed the exuberance and release of throwing and pounding clay. And I needed a creative outlet for my unexpressable feelings. I've never resented the money I borrowed to go to school, but I do resent the money and time spent on psychotherapy."

How did you get the job?

"I just started doing all this stuff, and when they came to me and told me they thought it was a little strange that I was doing all this work for free, I agreed with them, and asked for a salary. They felt guilty enough to give me one, and I gave notice the next day. Then I went home and had a suit burning ceremony. It smelled like hell and set off all the smoke alarms, but I needed to do it."

The Nike Approach: Just Do It

One person we interviewed called this the Zen approach to job hunting. Start doing something, and it will become your job. Kate, the potter, is an example of the effectiveness of the *Flashdance* approach ("take your passion, and make it happen").

People will want to know that you are dedicated and reliable. You are the best source of this information. And the best way to convey this information is not to say, but to do.

There is, as always, some danger here. If you work for free, some people will be reluctant to pay you. And, in some cases, if you start working without any guidance or instruction, you'll pick up some bad habits that you'll have to unlearn later. Not to mention that people who are getting paid to work often get pissed off at people who are hanging around doing the same work for free.

But there seems to be a value to doing something, rather than nothing. Freud said something to the effect that to be normal, you needed to be capable of loving and working. (No—we will not cite the German text and discuss all the shadings of its meaning; school is out!) Who knows what normal is, but it does seem that a lot of people are happier when they're doing something, and that happier people are more likely to get hired. So, there is logic, of a sort, to the idea of "just doing it."

How to Make Use of a Useless Degree

JOIN UP

Instead of looking at the decision of what to do as just a job decision, you could look at it as a lifestyle decision, and decide to join a group where your job and your social life are tightly entwined.

Before you do it, however, think about it long and hard. You can lose a lot of freedom when you sign up with certain groups. They'll start to tell you what you can wear, how long your hair should be, and perhaps even whom you can marry and what you should think. And some groups, like the military for example, work hard to keep you from leaving before you've served the full term that you signed up for.

28 🦉 Army

Butch is in the Army. He is working at a base on the East Coast.

"I hadn't really thought about joining the military until senior year. I wish I had. I could have saved a lot of money through ROTC. But I wasn't ready. But senior year I got into a little trouble during spring break, and it became clear to me that, whatever I had learned in college, I hadn't learned discipline. And it was pretty clear that I was going to need it.

"I didn't have a clue as to what kind of work I could do, where I wanted to live—nothing. So the military kind of made sense. It's not the way I pictured it. I doubt I'll ever see any combat. But I am part of what I believe to be the most miraculous institution on earth. Even if we don't fight, we deter.

"Some of my classmates have given me grief about spending four years developing my mind and then joining an institution where I have to take orders. It's not like that. I'm learning things that just weren't taught in college. I'm gaining maturity, learning to lead as well as to follow, and learning to get along with a much broader spectrum of people than I ever saw on campus.

"Plus there's the physical aspect. If I'd stayed on the road I was on, I'd have died of a heart attack by age forty-five. Now I'm going to be in perfect shape at that age, and entitled to a full pension. I can start a whole second life then.

"Think of it this way. My teeth needed work. The Army fixed them. What company would do that? Sure, some of the stuff we have to do is bullshit, but it all helps us learn to work as a team."

"It's not a hard job to get. Call the number in the commercials, or walk into the local recruiting office. It does help to have an idea of what service you want to be in most."

Make Your Own Lists

There are all sorts of lists of jobs. Jobs that pay the most. Professions given the most respect. Jobs with the best future. They're interesting, but not generally helpful. It probably doesn't matter to you that accountants suffer from little stress if you hate numbers, or that professional basketball players make good money if you are five feet tall and can't dribble. It won't help you to know about the best cities for jobs if you are unwilling to move.

Make your own lists. Jobs you've heard about. Jobs you want. Jobs that are available in the area you want to live in. Those lists will be much more relevant and helpful.

29   Kibbutznik

Sarah lives on a kibbutz in Israel.

"Being on a kibbutz gives my life meaning. Until you've been on one, you have no understanding of Middle East politics. Live on one and you'll know why Israel will be forever. We are scratching our lives out of the desert. We rely on each other. We will never give up. We cannot be beaten. We have destiny and right on our side. I am playing a small part in reclaiming the Holy Land. I am not studying history; I am part of it.

"The kibbutz is a much more sensible social structure than the family. The duties of raising children are shared. Children grow up much less screwed up. They have a sense of community and a sense of duty. They grow up with more resources and more skills. They have fewer issues when a parent dies or when they grow away.

"You would think my parents would be proud, but they hate it. I'm too far away, and they say they didn't send me to college to be a farmer. Too bad. This is my life. I'll never go back to being the vain tennis star mall rat they were so proud of."

How did you get the job?

"I had a pen pal. I went to visit her. It was supposed to be just a tourist trip, but it turned out to be more. I fell in love with the country, the struggle, and the people. And I fell in love with a soldier with the deepest eyes I had ever seen. I came back to the U.S. for a while, but my heart never left Israel."

Employment as Musical Chairs

Since much of the unemployment in this country is structural unemployment—unemployment that's part of how the system works and fine-tunes itself—being unemployed is not a reflection on you. To some extent, unemployed workers are like reserve soldiers, waiting to be thrown into the battle. The government's idea of the ideal level of unemployment has risen over the years. It used to be that 3 percent unemployment was unacceptable. Now 6 percent is considered to be reasonable.

The employment picture is like a game of musical chairs. Every time the music stops, a chair is removed. The winners are the people who grab a place, but the others are needed to make the game interesting.

On kibbutzes, on the other hand, the structure is different. It is designed so that all members of the community work. It's structural full employment.

30 🦉 Commune Member

Joss lives on a commune.

"I think that people who buy society's assumptions about working and how to live have missed the whole point of a liberal education. If you really believe in change and progress, living in an intentional community seems like a logical response.

"What I do to earn money is, in the end, a relatively irrelevant question. Better questions are *How do I relate to the earth?, Do I tread lightly?, Am I seeking enlightenment?*

"Getting a job, earning money, and spending it essentially perpetuates a sick system. We concentrate on being freer by needing less, and sharing what we have. Don't increase income, decrease need. Don't replace, repair. There is an honor to honest labor that's lost when it's turned into dollars. Much of what we do is done for barter.

"We are not only living a reasoned, examined, justifiable life, we are also exploring a model for how people will have to live in coming centuries. It's clear to everyone who takes the time to free themselves from the brainwashing of the mass media that the American dream is doomed. As Lily Tomlin said, 'The problem with the rat race is that even if you win, you're still a rat.' We're learning how to be humans, not rats."

How did you get into this commune?

"A friend brought me out here on the night of a full moon for a drumming festival around a bonfire. The next morning I told one of the women here that I had this strange, calm feeling of having come home. She told me I had."

West Coast Point of View

On the West Coast, more than on the East Coast or in the middle of the country, people are introduced by what they're interested in, not by what they do. Someone who's introduced as a Deadhead may well turn out to be a computer programmer. Since we're all likely to be changing careers three or more times, we should try and go more toward the West Coast model for social interaction and self-image.

Just because someone changes jobs or careers doesn't mean that their identity changes. And just because someone is out of work or between jobs doesn't mean their identity has disappeared or dimmed.

Of course, until you've found a job, *you'll* be pretty interested in knowing where everyone works.

RESEARCH

At some point in school you probably had to do some research: look a few things up, maybe ask a few questions, or make a few observations. In other words, research is a skill you already have. And, in our research-based economy, there are lots of jobs that involve research skills.

31   Private Detective

Shelly isn't your image of a private detective. She doesn't wear a fedora or chain smoke. In fact, she has an unassuming demeanor that makes you trust her and helps her blend into almost any crowd. And that's what makes her so good. Her average assignment isn't trailing toughs onto a tanker in a foggy harbor, it's renting a car in a strange city and reporting whether the local franchise kept the office well lit, the car neat and in good repair, and the paperwork filled in properly, and whether she was overcharged or talked down to because she is a woman.

"I also do a lot of asset research for divorce cases. It's not cloak-and-dagger stuff. Mostly searching computer databases and local papers and business journals in various libraries to track down hidden wealth. Turns out that half of the guys getting divorced have found clever ways to put their dollars out of reach. It feels good when you find out that some guy who's crying poor owns a business in the Bahamas or a condo in Colorado or a fat Swiss bank account."

How did you get the job?

"My divorce lawyer got me the job so I could afford to pay him. Honest. And yes, I did check up on my ex. He was cheating, but not monetarily. But Lord help him if he ever stops the support payments. I'll be back in court in a second."

Customize

Thanks to the wonders of technology, it's relatively quick and easy to customize a resumé so it's targeted at the place or person you're sending it to.

If you're applying for a research job, be sure to include the research component of all the projects you did at school. If the person you'll be interviewing with went to your college, devote more space to college activities. If it's a secretarial position you're trying for, list how fast you type and all the software you know how to use.

Customizing your resumé gives you an advantage over competitors who don't—as long as you design it well, or, better yet, have someone design it for you, and use a good laser printer. Just be sure to save all your old copies on computer disk—you never know when you'll need them.

32   Market Research

Gwen works for a large "packaged goods" company—a company that makes nationally advertised brands that are sold in supermarkets.

"We research everything here. The stakes are so high for a national brand that there's no way we want to launch a loser. We test products, positionings, ad concepts and executions, and packing. We run focus groups, phone intercepts, mall intercepts, test markets—you name it. And we have all sorts of secondary data on stuff like brand awareness, brand share, share of voice that we track. We even subscribe to reports from futurists. When a decision is made around here, it has a strong factual basis.

"I thought research was going to be a quiet, organized backroom function. It's not. We're doing presentations all the time, and we're always being rushed for toplines—early results—by brand managers with agendas who are always misinterpreting our results. I don't really know as much as I should about the mathematical models that we use, but I have a decent sense of what looks right, which is more than you can say for most of the executives here. Most of the heavy analysis and number crunching is done by outside suppliers, anyway."

How did you get the job?

"My roommate's father is a big executive at the company. They have a no nepotism policy that keeps him from getting her hired, but he was able to put in a good word for me. And because I'm both female and nonwhite, I gave them two more points toward their diversity goals."

Knowledge Workers

It may not seem that way right now, but "the knowledge workers"—people who deal with information—are among the few groups who are supposed to come out OK as the job market keeps evolving. If you're a knowledge worker, it will be hard to bring samples of what you make home to the family, but you're more likely to be able to keep your job.

Basically, a "knowledge worker" is an intermediary between all the data that's building up in computers and the people who want to make decisions based on that data. Knowledge workers not only enter data, transfer it from computer to computer, and retrieve it, they also take that raw data and select it, format it, massage it, chart it, interpret it, and project it, so that it goes from being a whole bunch of raw data to being a small piece of easily digested and used information. (People keep saying that computers will do this by themselves and that executives will start using their own terminals to get this kind of information for themselves. But to set up a system so this can happen, often the data has to be encoded in new ways and reentered, which creates a lot of work for knowledge workers.)

Because they control this data, knowledge workers have become strangely powerful in some corporations. In ancient times, generals visited oracles to see if the omens were good

---

for a military campaign; now senior vice presidents visit knowledge workers to see if the omens are good for a product launch and a merger.

33 🦉 Paralegal

Bernadette is a paralegal. She spends all day getting information and references for lawyers.

"The coolest thing about my job is that I get to do some work with lawyers who are doing pro bono work on capital punishment cases. I'm very involved in that cause. It's absolutely ridiculous to think that we, a supposedly civilized country, still execute people. In most of the cases, when you look into them, the person about to die was poorly defended and denied many rights. They are being rushed to their death because politicians don't want to seem soft on crime. And the deterrent argument is bullshit; it doesn't hold up. My work has helped save a few lives—how many people can say that?

"But whether the case interests me or not, what I do is very meticulous, dedicated research. The law firm interprets 'due diligence' as meaning they have to have explored every possible citation in every court in every state that may have some bearing on a case in the past, the present, or the future. And some of the lawyers just love to trip you up. They'll ask for information when they already know the answer, just to see how good you are.

"The pay isn't bad, although I only get a fraction of what they charge for my time. The lawyers know I'm smart, and they'll ask that I handle projects they really care about, but I'll always be a second-class citizen in their minds. I took the job so I could figure out if I wanted to be a lawyer. I don't. And I wouldn't go out with a lawyer, either. What's the point of trying to relate to someone who has been trained to always argue, even when they know they're not right?"

"One of the senior lawyers—a married man—picked me up in a bar. I got his business card and the name of someone in Personnel from him. I contacted Personnel and introduced myself as a personal friend of his—what's he going to say? I had a good degree. I wore the right silly St. Laurie suit with the floppy woman's tie and the shoes that were sensible, but clearly a bit sexy and expensive. I dressed for the part; I got the job. One of the partners saw me on the street once with my nose ring in, which I don't wear to work, and he nearly fell over."

Are You Looking for a Job or Not?

Some of the manuals on networking tell you to go around reassuring people that you are not quite yet looking for a job. This is, of course, a lie. Even worse, it's an obvious lie. Worse still, it's a stupid thing to say.

The reason books tell you to say that is so that you won't scare people and make them feel pressured. If they don't think you're looking for a job, and just think you feel they're incredibly fascinating, they'll be happy to spend time with you, and you can pick their brains, and maybe in the process they'll also offer you a job.

The problem is, many executives have read these books themselves. They know what you're up to. They know the script. They may have even been through it. And they may not feel they have the time or the tolerance to waste on having you stare earnestly into their eyes and take notes as you work your way up to the questions "Is there anyone else you would recommend I talk to as part of my research efforts? Can you give me the names, nicknames, and direct phone line numbers for three people who could hire me?" We spoke to one executive who delights in telling people who use the "I'm not looking for a job yet" approach that

he can't waste his time on them because he's busy interviewing and hiring people who are ready to work.

It's going to be easier to be honest with people. Admit
that you're looking for work, but reassure them that you
don't necessarily expect *them* to give you a job, and that
you'll only take a few minutes of their valuable time.

34 🦉 Freelance Research

Helen is doing freelance research. She thinks of the New York
Public Library as her office.

"Maybe it's because I didn't know I was adopted until I was
eleven, but I hate secrets. And I like the fact that I can discover things. Most of my work recently has been going to the
library for a book packager and assembling research files that
they hand to the writers. It's basically a matter of finding the
right books and periodicals and xeroxing the relevant sections.
It's kind of archaic—I could get them much of the same information via an on-line Nexis or Lexis search, but it's what
they want.

"I'm doing this freelance, which I love. When I was in-house
at the research firm I was always getting talked into adminis-
tering phone questionnaires, tabulating results, preparing
presentation charts, and collating reports. I hated all that stuff.
Now, essentially, I feel like I never left school, like I'm still
working on a thesis.

"I also make a lot more per hour. The people who hire me
have very low expectations. They have no idea how fast I can
work. It's not that I'm making a lot more in total. But I no
longer have to waste time in the morning wandering around
an office like a zombie. I'm no good in the morning. Never
have been; never will be. I hit the library promptly at noon
with the paper read and a couple of latte grandes in me, and
I just tear until five."

"This current assignment I got by talking to a guy waiting for the copier at the library. He told me what he was doing, and I asked him if they were hiring others. He told me what to say when I went in to speak to the research director, and took me in to meet him. We share a lot of assignments, so he gets stuff for me and I get stuff for him."

Medical Insurance Tactics

Most full-time college students get some sort of medical coverage as part of their college tuition. Lots of college-age people are covered by their parents' policies; and lots aren't. Not being insured is risky, and it can make you cautious. Helen wouldn't go skiing or ice skating while she wasn't insured. Her family had been hit by enough medical bills, and she wasn't willing to take the risk.

And being underinsured is almost as bad. One person we talked to reported "I thought I was insured. But it wasn't much of a policy. I paid thousands of dollars for postoperative rehabilitative therapy for my hand, which I had injured while renovating my house. The insurance company refused to cover it because the therapy was conducted in the Occupational Therapy Department and they didn't cover occupational therapy. They refused to acknowledge that the care was postoperative care; they said it was marked 'occupational,' and even though it had nothing to do with my occupation, they wouldn't pay for even part of it. They were incredibly uncooperative, although they did pay for part of the surgery itself. The injury set me back, and so did paying for it."

Medical insurance is expensive. And since getting meaningful national health care reform seems highly unlikely, the first thing you might want to do is find out how long your college will cover you for. The next question is how long you can stay on your parents' policy. Yes, this may seem degrading—but it's better than being uninsured.

WRITE

Another marketable skill you may have is writing. Remember all those term papers? All those themes in English class? All those reports? Odds are, you've done a lot of writing.

There are lots of ways to sell your services as a writer. You probably can't get a lot for your services until you've developed a track record and perhaps an area or two of specialization. But, take it from us, it's rewarding work, with no heavy lifting.

35 🦉 Freelance Writer

Woody is a freelance writer. He works out of his home, or out of people's offices.

"Most writers in America are starving because they look on writing as a hobby or therapy, not as a business. I'm making it because I will write anything I can get paid for. Sure, I'd like to sit at home, sip tea, and work on poems, stories, novels, and screenplays—but I'd be evicted for nonpayment of rent.

"In the past year, I have written a set of clues that got you pieces to a puzzle that was used at a sales meeting to keep salesmen involved, a direct mail piece for a local contractor, a speech for a fund-raiser, an instruction manual for an electronic gizmo, and a sales presentation. Plus I've done my share of proofreading for other people.

"I love the term freelance. It brings up this image of a knight galloping around the countryside fighting heroic battles. Nothing could be further from the truth. I say I'm a writer—but I spend pitifully little time writing. Most of the time I'm interviewing, schmoozing, doing homework, organizing, revising, and begging for payment.

"One thing that people should know about writing is that it's addictive. Once you get good at it, you want to keep doing it. There's a real thrill to figuring out the right way to communicate a message. It never gets easy, but it does get somewhat easier. In my spare time I write for charities on a pro bono basis. Not because I have to, but because I can.

"Another thing that people need to know is not to get too attached to their work. No matter how good it is, it will be edited. And not always for the better, except in the sense that better is anything that gets you closer to getting paid. Everyone thinks they're a writer, or at least an editor.

"The final thing is that your computer will become more

important to you than your car. You have to treat it lovingly, but never trust it. Back up everything."

How did you get the job?

"I gave myself the job of writer. Or maybe it's just what I was meant to do. In a primitive society, I would have been a *griot*— a storyteller. I got my first work by the classic marketing technique of giving away free samples. I went into people's offices and asked to do an assignment for free. Most people were weirded out by it, which was depressing—I couldn't give my work away—but some took me up on it. And if business got really slow, I'd give away more free samples."

Joys of Working at Home

- No office politics.
- No one sees what you wear—you can have important phone conversations while naked!
- You can play whatever music you want.
- No need for a bathroom key—and no one in the next stall.
- The coffee is generally better.
- No one can find you to collect for birthday and retirement parties.
- No commuting.
- You get to read your personal mail in the middle of the day.
- You can accept delivery of all of your packages; no more Saturday trips to the post office to claim them.
- You have an excuse for stocking up on all sorts of office supplies.
- No fire drills.

36 🦉 Pornography

Sy is a writer. What he doesn't tell people at first is what he writes. He writes pornography.

"I'm not a great writer, but I have no inhibitions and I know how to follow a formula. Pornography publishers don't turn out to be a particularly imaginative lot. Find out the taboos before you start; each publisher knows what acts he'll publish and which he won't. If you don't know the taboos, you might waste a bunch of time describing a perversion that your publisher won't print. Get a copy of something they like, and pound away at the keyboard making variations on it.

"Use a pseudonym, and tell your relatives you are writing for foreign publications that don't send review copies. Don't tell friends because they will want to submit stories and samples to you, and you don't want to know your friends that well, trust me on that. Never make the people resemble your lovers and never exactly describe anything you've actually done. Your lover *will* read it, and will object to it. I wrote about making love on acid, and the woman in question recognized it and got all bent out of shape at a description of her breasts as two perfect giant sunny-side-up eggs. She never forgave me—and that was about the calmest description I'd ever used.

"For the record, you don't have to do a lot of research. You don't actually have to have done all this stuff. I suspect that some of the porno writers out there are priests and nuns working out their frustrations, or using what they've heard in confession. And, for the most part, porno writing is profoundly unerotic for the writer. It's pretty repetitive, and the publishers frown on surprise outcomes."

How did you get the job?

"A friend and I stayed up all night one night writing what we thought was the ultimate porno story. The next day I went down to the magazine office and demanded they buy it. They didn't. But they told me what kind of stuff they would accept, and told me to come back. I think they liked the idea that some hip kid wanted to contribute—it made them all feel younger. And I was real cheap. I've been edging my rates up, and no one's complained. I deliver."

Hassles of Working at Home

- No human interaction.
- No mailroom.
- No free coffee.
- No "attaboys" from your coworkers.
- You have to answer your home phone respectably.
- Half the calls you pick up are annoying telemarketers— and you're so lonely you talk to them.
- Office supplies are insanely expensive.
- There's nothing between you and a nap.
- You have to clean up before clients come over.
- No one to pick up the ball if you drop it.
- No commuting excuses.
- Housemates and houseguests will interrupt your work.
- The TV is always there to tempt you.
- The refrigerator is always there to tempt you.
- No office mates to blame things on.

37 🦉 Advertising Copywriter

Coby works at an ad agency. In fact, he almost lives there.

"Everyone thinks they could write ads better than what's out there, but I'm the guy who was arrogant and confident enough to *know* that I could. I had attitude, and I built a killer portfolio. My book had ads in it that would take people's breath away. It took me over a year of moonlighting with art directors to get my book that solid. And I still couldn't get hired.

"But now that I've been at a few different agencies, I'm building a name for myself, and I get recruiting calls. I listen carefully. This isn't a business for old people; it's a business where you have to rise fast and retire before you become a pathetic wreck living on past glory. But I won't go to just any agency. I want to be at a place where the creative department rules, with good clients.

"The irony is that after all I did to get into this business, I'm not sure I can stay in it. I know I'm good, but everything I do gets compromised. Our clients have no guts. And agency people are losing what little balls they once had. No one remembers what it's like to be young. I may move on to film or some other area where I can have more creative control."

How did you get the job?

"I decided to do anything I had to do to get inside an ad agency. I got a job as an assistant secretary to the head of the creative department. I am a wicked fast typist, and there's this status thing for some women where they want a male secretary as a reverse gender role thing. It was a good place to be. I knew everything that was going on and got to look at all the work that came in.

"When an emergency hit where the agency president wanted an extra campaign to show a new business prospect that the agency could do young, wacky creative, a junior art director and I worked the whole weekend on storyboards for a cable-TV-only campaign that made MTV look like "Romper Room." The creative director would have killed it, so we had to pull a fast one and make sure the president saw it first. It was ballsy, but the president, who's an old fart, likes to think he's one of the young set, so he bought it, even though he didn't really get it.

"The agency head introduced me in the meeting as a copywriter, and no one corrected him. The campaign was produced and I used it to get a job at another agency. I couldn't stay where I was: they still thought of me as a secretary, and the senior creative folks were really pissed that I had showed them up, and they were just waiting for a chance to get back at me. I had broken the sacred chain of spending ages doing dumb collateral—brochures, mailers and signs, and trade ads—and jumped straight into TV."

Moving Target

If your Uncle Blair asks you why you're having trouble finding employment, tell him that things today are changing so quickly that finding a job is like hitting a moving target.

In the old days people used to joke about buggy whip companies—a kind of business made obsolete by the automobile. But that change took decades to happen. Now technology and cultural change are making businesses obsolete in a matter of years.

Imagine if you were a genius at making 45 RPM plastic records. Or if you were the absolute best at designing 8-track stereo cartridges. Or a CB-radio repair specialist. Or a disco instructor. Or a manufacturer of dial telephones.

Jobs are now fluid. If you had gone out and researched jobs in high school, and dedicated your whole college career to aiming at a specific job in a specific company, it's quite possible that the job you were aiming for would have been eliminated by the time you got out of college. Even if the skill you learned was still in demand, the company could have moved, or eliminated the particular position you were aiming at.

Your mission, should you decide to accept it (and you don't have much choice), is to try and hit a moving target. That makes your job harder. But it also raises the possibility that other moving targets will swing into your sights.

38 🦉 PR Writer

Peggy is a public relations writer who works at a high technology company. That's about a tenth of what she does, but it's as good a description as she's got.

"I'm not the world's best writer, but I know my field. High tech has a language all its own, and a context all its own. I couldn't begin to write in the food or sporting goods industry, but the writers in those industries would never understand what we're saying here. It would take them a month just to learn the acronyms, and a year to get a feel for the technologies and how they relate. Certain companies own specific terms and positions; you don't want to use a competitor's metaphor; you want to top it.

"When we plan a new system (we never say 'product' or 'machine' or 'equipment'), I am integrally involved with every aspect of the launch. I contribute to the meetings where the positioning is worked out, sit in the meetings where we name the system—Should we call it a name, like Excellence, or a number like XL 77777?—write all the releases and personally pitch the story to the editors and consultants, all of whom I know. I write the executives' speeches, rehearse them for questions at press conferences, and write the articles that show up in magazines with their names on them.

"I take a lot of flak for the company. People in the high tech world play fast and loose with the truth. They announce products before they know they can make them. They claim capabilities that they know will not be available for years, and they almost always miss their dates. There are a lot of 'virtual products,' products that are almost there, and a lot of faked demos where they rig a box with lights to show what the planned product will do. A lot of times we'll rush an announcement just so we can one-up a competitor whose announcement was probably fake, too. All of this leaves me doing a lot of tap dancing, backpedaling, hemming and hawing with editors who believed me. Of course, we're no worse than anyone else.

"And the editors are only part of the problem. Consultants are also key. They recommend a lot of systems, and their evaluations have direct impact on stock prices and capital availability. So we have to suck up to them, and they always want exclusive audiences with the top people—who then make promises they can't keep—and an inside look at our long-range plans and vision.

"Plus there are the customers. The user group is really dangerous because they actually know what we can deliver and what we can't. They bought on the basis of promises, and we have to manage their expectations and their reactions so that they are reasonably happy and don't go about badmouthing us. Especially the Beta-site customers who test drive the early releases of new systems. We call them the bleeding edge.

"I write scripts for all these scenarios. How to answer this question and that. They never get printed or published, but they keep our CEO from standing there with his jaw open and a surprised look on his face."

How did you get the job?

"I went and talked to all the editors at the computer and communications trade magazines. One of them was aware of an opening and sent me over. They had fired the last guy for telling the truth.

"I met with the VP, Corporate Communications, who would have met with anyone the editor sent over because he needed the editor to be nice to the company. He did most of the talking. In the midst of the interview, the CEO blew into the office and started talking a blue streak about the positioning they really needed, and why the current position was limiting. When the CEO stopped, the VP stalled for time by asking me what I thought. I basically paraphrased some of the CEO's spiel back to him, and everyone thought I was brilliant.

"I had to meet with a spooky Human Resources guy who played all sorts of word games with me, and fill out a bunch of forms agreeing to their checking me out and to a pre-employment physical. But it was basically meaningless. The

CEO had liked me and liked the idea of a bright, young female PR person. I was in."

Headhunt the Headhunters

Most headhunters—recruiters, placement firms, search specialists—will not give a damn about you. You are too green, too inexperienced. They can't make enough money off of placing you. They will try and send you to temp agencies. But be persistent. Get in to talk to them. Network with them. Make friends with them. It's easy—most of them are in the business because they're friendly and get along well with other people. Find out who's who in the industry you're looking at. Ask them for the names of three people they placed, and go talk to them. And, once you've found a job, let them know where you are. Once you're experienced and employed, they may find you your next job.

39 Journalist

Cheri is a journalist. She's on her fourth job in her fourth city in four years. She doesn't care. Wherever there's a newspaper or news magazine office, she feels at home.

"I guess I'm a typical story. I wrote for the school paper. Had a great faculty adviser who changed my life. Thought I'd be Woodward and Bernstein and Edward R. Murrow all rolled into one. Hit New York, and had to start as a fact checker. But I'm writing again. Can't imagine doing anything else.

"Once you become a journalist, you do it all the time. Look for the real story behind the one you're told. Figure out if it's important for people to know what's really going on. Work on phrasing it in a way that will make it simple to understand, but preserve all the important complexities. Present all sides, but still maintain your capacity for outrage.

"If it weren't for the fact that there is a certain camaraderie among journalists, I'd have no social life at all. It just doesn't work. I get obsessional about a story, and whoever I'm going out with starts to feel ignored. And forget living with me. Some nights I don't come home at all. And it drives guys nuts when I start asking them questions the way I'm trained to do. They either say I'm paranoid or claim that I don't trust them.

"The oddest thing that has happened to me so far is being sued. I wrote some things about a pseudo-science cult that the cult didn't like. The stories were all true. I had done my research well, and could back up everything I wrote. But this outfit has a pattern of trying to silence criticism with lawsuits. They've got a lot of writers intimidated. I figured I was just the person to go after them: I have nothing they can sue me for. There was a lot more at risk for my magazine, who got sued, too, of course—but, to their credit, they printed it."

How did you get the job?

"You've got to use the same doggedness and thoroughness you'd use as a journalist. Find the jobs, find the decision makers, find their levers, and push them. Do your homework before you come in. I got this job through the journalist's grapevine—there is still some esprit de corps. I got my first one by volunteering to be a stringer for my hometown paper."

The Clip Catch-22

In most jobs it's the "Experience Catch-22": you can't get a job without experience and you can't get experience without a job. In journalism it's the "Clip Catch-22": you can't get a job without clips—published samples—but how are you going to get clips without a job?

The answer is that the clips don't have to be professional ones. If you wrote for the school paper, you're in good shape. Even assignments from a journalism class will do. But you need clips. (Yes, there are a few cases where people have talked their way into journalism jobs by offering to do

How to Make Use of a Useless Degree

hazardous assignments for free—but it's a very, very long shot. Even if you're working for free, the publication still has a reputation to uphold, and people at publications generally feel that they're too busy to put themselves in positions where they'll have to hand-hold an amateur through a crisis.)

If you have no samples, set about getting some. Write for the church newsletter, or for your school's alumni newsletter. Take a journalism course. Be a stringer for any publication that will let you. Just get writing, and save everything that gets published.

40 🦉 Technical Writer

Evelyne writes software manuals for personal computer programs.

"Technical writing isn't just spreadsheet writing. It can be fascinating. I do a lot of writing for graphics packages, and there are real challenges involved in making the manuals work.

"I spend a lot of my time with the people who actually developed the programs. Some are guru-types who are brilliant but incredibly inarticulate—only they don't know it. Most of the time it's easier to ask them to show you how to do something than it is to ask them to explain it. And it's much, much better to go over stuff in person as opposed to over the phone.

"It's intense work. When I'm finishing up a book, I turn into a hermit and won't answer the phone. It calls for lots of discipline and an unstoppable drive to organize. And you have to keep reminding yourself of how little the readers know, and how easy it would be to bore them or lose them."

How did you get the job?

"My case isn't typical. I never said, Today I'll be a manual writer. It just happened. I already had a writing background, and a woman I knew became a production manager at a company and asked me if I could write a manual. Once I'd written one, there were people who were begging me to write others. If I were just starting, I'd blanket the market with resumés. Companies are desperate for technical writers.

Job Shock

If you've never been fully employed and self-supporting, your first job is likely to provide you with some nasty surprises. Here are a few that people have mentioned:

- You have no free time.
- You have no spare energy.
- You have no independence.
- Getting the laundry done becomes exciting.
- You start having to know and care about taxes.
- You start having to know and care about insurance.
- There is no student union—and shopping, cooking, and cleaning take a lot of time.
- You have to pay to go to a gym.
- You have to schedule a social life—you and your pals aren't together in classes and in the library.
- Although you're making money, you have less of it to spend.

How to Make Use of a Useless Degree

41 🦉 Desktop Publishing

Ben writes, designs, and "publishes" a newsletter for a small company that wants to look bigger.

"There's a saying that 'on the Internet, no one knows you're a dog.' Same thing with doing a newsletter—no one has to know how young you are, how dingy your apartment is, or how straggly you look. I am, arguably, the most knowledgeable writer in a tiny, tiny corner of business.

"Down the road, I think I'll be able to draw enough lessons out of what I've learned about this industry to write a book about it, and perhaps sell myself as a consultant.

"I do everything I can by telephone. I interview my clients, their suppliers, their customers, and industry experts. I call lobbyists, whatever. And, every two months, I put out a newsletter that gets mailed out to a few thousand people.

"My apartment is dominated by the computer. I've got a humongous monitor because you really need to be able to see a whole spread in actual size when you design a newsletter. Originally, I just wrote the copy and the firm gave it to a designer who worked with their printer. But the charges were incredible. I do the design work for a fraction of what they were paying, and it's good extra income for me.

"The biggest hassle is filing space. I keep all my records on disk, but I still get a lot of brochures, articles, videotapes that I want to keep for reference. And there's all sorts of correspondence I need to file. Not only are file cabinets incredibly expensive, they take up a lot of room; but they'd be better than having everything in cartons from the liquor store.

"In theory, I could start doing another newsletter in a related or totally different industry. It wouldn't be hard; I've already climbed the learning curve. But I'm just too lazy right now. This is a great gig, and I have no interest in working full-time."

"I started talking to people in this company when I was doing my thesis. I was writing about environmental legislation and its impact on small companies, and they were a perfect example. I had spoken to the president, and he asked me to send him a copy of my thesis when it was done.

"He called me to discuss some of what I'd written, and asked me to write a white paper that he could send out to his 'stakeholders.' That became the first issue of the newsletter."

Buzzword Alert

"Excellence," "quality," and "teams" are words that some business people practically worship. If someone uses them during an interview, it's a reasonable bet that these are important concepts for the person talking. Ask them to elaborate. "Teams" might be a particularly good sign, because it might mean that you could get put into a work environment where you work closely with experienced experts who will teach and mentor you. Ideally, the team structure could let you advance faster.

On the other hand, "teams" could also be a code word for "reorganizing people into teams so they'll be more productive and we can fire a lot of people." For the most part, the words "downsizing," "decruiting," "rightsizing," "reengineering," "outplacement," and even "rethinking" or "reinventing" mean that job cutting is going on.

The fact that job cutting is going on doesn't mean that a company's not hiring. A lot of times a company will be clearing out "deadwood" and replacing the people who leave with younger, more flexible people who will do more for less.

TRAVEL

It used to be that a young man wasn't considered educated until he had taken a "Grand Tour" of Europe. Those days are long gone. But there's still a lot of reasons to travel, and a lot of reasons to want to travel while you are still young and (relatively) free.

Travel is, of course, expensive. But there are some ways to combine it with work.

42 🦉 Air Courier

Bill is an air courier. It's not really a job, but it's a way to get free airfare.

"All the kids I went to college with seem to have traveled all over the world. I always felt like I was the only one who hadn't been anywhere. Now I'm making up for it with a vengeance. When a corporation needs to send something somewhere in a rush, I fly there for free—the only requirement is that all I can take is carry-on luggage. They use my luggage allowance to ship the stuff.

"I spent my life working hard to get into college, and to survive college. I know I'll have to work hard again soon. But, in the meanwhile, I want to live a little, to learn to be a little more spontaneous. It's a real challenge to find yourself in a strange city and to figure out how to amuse yourself and how to get around. When I'm through this phase, maybe I'll get a job that involves a lot of travel, maybe I won't. But at least I'll never again have to look at my shoes and mumble that I've never been anywhere and never had any adventures.

"Once I get someplace, I can stay as long as I want before using the return part of the ticket. Of course, that could be expensive. So I stay in hostels or with friends. A lot of those well-traveled folks from school are working abroad. In return, they can crash with me in New York.

"In between trips I temp. I've also been pitching stories to travel magazines, so I can become a travel writer, and get free airfare and lodgings that way. I'd like to write a book on how to travel cheaply and find unexpected delights. I'm becoming an expert at that."

I got a passport and I registered, for fifty dollars, with an outfit called Now, Voyager here in New York. When I'm ready to travel, I call their hotline to see what trips are available.

Justifications for Travel Jobs

If you take a job that involves a lot of travel, or if you decide just to travel for a while, some people will think you're being self-indulgent—especially Uncle Donovan. Maybe you are. But there are also good strategic reasons for traveling.

All indications are that import/export businesses will play a growing role in our economy over the next several years. There's hardly a big company in the United States that hasn't started talking about its global orientation and its entry into global markets. Having traveled, and being willing to travel, makes you more attractive to these companies. The more you've traveled, the better equipped you are to deal with other countries and cultures.

This can be a great excuse for going to out-of-the-way countries. There are lots of people around who know something about France, Scotland, Germany, and Italy. But there are fewer who are familiar with Burkina Faso, Myanmar, or the provinces of China. Of course, you can't always expect luxury when you get off the beaten track, and there may be strange political things to deal with. (If, for example, you go into Zimbabwe saying you're a journalist, they'll put all sorts of extra restrictions on your visit.) But it would certainly set you apart from a lot of job applicants if you had firsthand knowledge of a couple of important, emerging markets.

43 🦉 English Instructor

Juan is teaching English in Japan. His parents' Christmas gift to him was a ticket to come home and visit them.

"The first thing to tell everybody is not to assume you'll be in the big city. I'm not in Tokyo. I'm in an industrial port city hours away. It's much less cultured and much less cosmopolitan. I really stand out there, and it's not always comfortable.

"What I've learned so far is that I really like America better. I don't like the beds, I don't like how much everything costs, I don't like being stared at for being tall, I don't like not being able to just talk to everyone in English. I miss hamburgers. But I think l had to come here to learn that.

"The finances are also not working out the way I had in mind. I thought I'd be able to save while being here. But everything is so expensive that I'll finish up as broke as when I started, without having been able to get to some of the other parts of Asia I wanted to tour.

"Meanwhile, I've learned more Japanese—language and manners—than I could ever have learned in the States, and I'm sure that will help me get a job when I come back. And I've learned something about myself."

How did you get the job?

"I answered an ad in the back of the college alumni magazine."

Quit or Get Fired?

When you know you're going to leave a job, often you have the choice of whether to quit or get fired. The act of quitting can be fun. You can take all your pent-up anger and act on it. You can do something that shows that they did not, in fact, own your soul. But quitting makes it harder for you to collect unemployment, and if you quit in an emotional rage, you're likely to "burn your bridges," and eliminate any chance of getting a good recommendation or working with the company in the future. There are ways to quit without offending people: imply that you'd like to stay, but you need to continue your studies, attend to some family business, etc.

Getting fired makes it easy to collect, but it can be painful to go through, and it looks bad on your record. Since most people at most companies feel bad about firing someone, you can often work out a deal where you leave "by mutual agreement" and retain the right to collect unemployment.

The words "laid off" are a nice compromise. They imply that you didn't quit, and that the company would have kept you if they could.

Clyde quit his job. The only problem is, he worked in a one-company town, and wasn't ready to move. That has made his ensuing life tough.

Barney quit in grand style and went to work for the competition. A year later, the companies merged, and he was again reporting to the manager he had told off.

44 Importer

Sophie's motto is "create your own fate." She likes to travel, and has a good eye for what she can resell at a profit.

"In Thailand, I bought thirty small wall-decor-size quilts made by Cambodian refugee women. I paid almost nothing for them. Believe me. I kept two, gave one to my parents and one to my sister, and sold the rest to a store for $60 apiece. I thought they were crazy, until I saw that they were selling them, no problem, for $145."

"So I thought about it, and I went to Central America and came back with string bags. Same kind of markup. Then I

How to Make Use of a Useless Degree

brought a bale of used kimonos back from Japan.

"I'm not exploiting anybody. I'm generally paying the appropriate price for the product in its local context. I'm exploiting the differential between the value placed on the goods where they're made and the value placed on them in the United States. I'm actually flirting with the idea of financing a woman's work cooperative in one of these countries. It doesn't take a lot of money, it would give me a steady supply of product, and I would be sponsoring small, sustainable growth in a country that needs it.

"The trick is to get away from the airports. The farther out into the country you go, the better the deals. And don't be in any kind of a rush: not to buy, and not for your stuff to arrive. Negotiating in a lot of the world is a very slow process, and the person who seems in a hurry gets taken. I'm always ready to walk away."

How did you get the job?

"Pure dumb luck. I didn't start out to be an importer. It never occurred to me; and it should have. I went through college wearing Indian saris and carrying Guatemalan string bags. But I can't resist a bargain. When I offered those quilts to the store, I was doing it to regain closet space, and I would have taken a lot less."

Doing Good and Being In Business

Don't assume you can't "do good" in private industry. The line between "business" and "doing good" is a lot blurrier than people assume. There are "socially responsible" investment firms, like Progressive Securities in Portland, Oregon, that specialize in advising people how to invest money in companies that meet whatever ethical standards the investor may hold. There are socially responsible mutual funds like Calvert, and money market funds like Working Assets. There are companies like Smith and Hawken, Ben &

Jerry's, and The Body Shop that are serious about what they call "cause-related marketing."

And you can choose to do business in "do good" ways. Sophie, for example, prefers to buy from women's cooperatives; if she funds one, she will be doing good and doing well at the same time.

Gene Moore, a former running back for the San Francisco Forty-Niners, runs a New York City–based company, Child Safety Communications, that creates safety training materials for parents and teachers to use with children. He says, "We're a for-profit enterprise, both because I have two kids to support, and because it's the fastest way for me to do the most good. We've created a promotional partnership with private companies that has already made and distributed three million copies of one guide. It would have taken ages to do that if we were a charity."

45 🦉 Au Pair

Heather is spending a year in Norway as an au pair. She came back to the U.S. to attend her graduation—she couldn't graduate with her class because she had to finish a paper, so she had to "walk" with the next year's class.

"Au pair—that's the international term for mother's helper. It's not rocket science, but it is a great way to really get to know a place and how people live there. It's totally unlike being a tourist. You get to know what people eat on a daily basis, how they play, how their appliances are different. How clean they keep things. How they express pleasure and pain. How they relate to the environment and to animals. What their real priorities are. Everything. It's not learning a language; it's learning a culture. And, believe me, this is a culture we could learn a lot from.

"I think it's good for the kids, too. They get exposed to another culture, at least a bit. If I ever have kids and can afford it, I'll certainly have an au pair.

"I think I've been remarkably lucky. I get along fabulously with the family I'm staying with. They even took me on vacation with them, which they didn't have to do. And I didn't have to go. But I went, which shows you how much we like each other. In fact, I don't know how I'll leave this job at the end of my year—I've become very attached to the girls.

"I've met some local people my age, so I'm getting out a bit and learning the non-family perspective, too. The people I work for are very solidly middle class, but there's a lot of diversity of political opinion among the other people I meet. And, while I'm pretty much a plain jane back home, here I'm a bit exotic."

How did you get the job?

"I contacted a placement service from an ad in my local newspaper. They screened me; I had to fill out a bunch of forms and have an interview and attend a seminar. Then they presented me to families looking for help, and made my travel arrangements."

Marrying into Money

A surprising number of males and females we spoke to were planning on pursuing what some call "the new G.I. plan: generous in-laws." It's certainly not a career path you have to go through college to try, but perhaps a degree makes you more marriageable.

When you get down to it, money is a pretty lousy reason for getting married, and it's likely to backfire in the long run. For one, there's no guarantee that those in-laws will want to support you. One person we talked to thought he had it made when he married into a family with a successful family business. He didn't expect to be supported, but he did expect a good job. It turned out that the family firm had experienced a bad situation with an in-law in the past, and had an unwritten rule against hiring spouses.

If you're still determined to try it, you might as well aim high: check out *Forbes'* annual 400-richest issue. It conveniently lists the marital status as well as the estimated worth of the richest of the rich.

46   Tour Guide

Joel gets all his travel paid for. The only drawback is that he has to drag a bunch of tourists along with him.

"Name the emergency, I've handled it. A tour member getting sick, one tour member fighting with another, people getting lost, people getting arrested. You panic the first time, but you get good at it.

"The salary is low, but you make money through tips and through kickbacks from the retailers. I know which restaurant and which gift shop to send my people to at every stop along the way. It's a bit sleazy, but it was in place when I started, and I'm not going to rock the boat.

"It all sounds very exotic, but it's not. It's just a job. It does have romantic possibilities, but none you'd want. People have this image of having a European fling, and I'm the closest available suspect. I've had advances from women whose husbands were also on the tour, from moony-eyed high schoolers, as well as from the occasional qualified candidate. I broke the rule once, and it ruined the group dynamics: all the guys were jealous of me, and all the girls were jealous of her. Of course I am willing to make arrangements to see people after the tours."

How did you get the job?

"When I was in high school, I went on a tour and I looked up to the leader and said, 'That's who I want to be.' The tour company closed the next year. After exams, I called all the tour groups advertised in the Sunday travel section and offered my services. I called them every Monday for seven weeks. On the seventh week, someone was desperate enough to hire me."

That's LIFO

If bald Uncle Howard wants to know what boneheaded (he should talk) thing you did that got you fired, tell him it was a simple matter of LIFO vs. Lifers.

LIFO is an inventory management term which stands for Last In, First Out. It's also how lots of companies handle cutbacks. If you take a job, and the company has to make cuts soon thereafter, the odds are you'll be one of the first to be fired, and the lifers, the people who have been at the company for a long time, will stay. It's not an irrational policy: the company has a lot invested in training the long-term employees. Besides, personnel policies are such that while firing a new employee costs a company just two weeks of salary, if that, firing a long-term employee costs the company months of severance pay.

On the other hand, you can always argue that the company is holding onto the people who got it in trouble in the first place. But arguing won't get you very far. If they have a LIFO policy and you're the newest, you'll be the first to go when there are cuts, regardless of how good you are.

47 🦉 Boat Person

All of Jed's worldly possessions, other than the few things of his he keeps on the yacht, are in storage. If you want to reach him, you call his answering service. He checks in each time he gets to a new marina.

"I have an incredible tan, I'm in good shape, and I spend a

lot of time on the water. I'm not making an incredible amount of money, but since the boat owner provides room, board, and most expenses, as well as salary, I'm banking most of what I make, so I won't have to work during the off season when the boat's hauled out for repairs.

"I've learned to keep a computer with me on the boat. It doesn't take up much space, and it lets me keep up correspondences. I also keep scuba equipment on board. I use it for checking the hull and the props, but I also use it for recreation. This boat's small, so I'm alone, but a lot of times there'll be several people in the standing crew. Even though it's small, it's nice. Good stereo, air conditioning, even a washer and dryer.

"The owner of this boat is older and a bit old-fashioned. When he's on board, I always wear a uniform and we're very careful about putting up and taking down the flag. I serve drinks and make and serve dinner and all that. But most of the time, I'm on here alone, moving the boat from harbor to harbor, waiting for the times when he can get away from his company.

"I wasn't always a boat person. At first I made the assumption that I couldn't make a living doing what I liked best— being on the water. I was wrong. There are a hundred ways to make a living on the water—and I've done a lot of them. I've taught people how to run their boats, moved boats up and down the East Coast for people, captained party cruises and whale watches, and even sold boats. To make it work, however, I had to be willing to give up dreams of a garden, dog, and stability."

How did you get the job?

"I got this job because I have a captain's license, but that's not where you start. You find your first boat job by doing anything you can to get onto a boat. My sister started out by hanging out at a marina bar and being there when a galley cook quit. They needed someone to ship out the next morning, and she was ready.

"After your first boat job, you just keep in touch with everyone you worked with and people from other boats you met up

How to Make Use of a Useless Degree

with. It's very fluid. I've hired people who later hired me. There are also boat personnel agencies in major port cities—but they want you to have experience."

Sectors and the Single Job Hunter

Economists keep saying that "the service sector" is the area in which the most new jobs will be created. Just what do they mean?

For most of them, "service" is the opposite of "goods," and what they're saying is that manufacturing jobs are being automated or being done out of the country, so service is what's left.

If you're flipping burgers and asking, "Want fries with that?" you're in services (low paying services). And if you're a high-powered marketing consultant, you're also in services.

If you build houses, you're not in services (although it's hard to imagine how this job will go overseas); but if you sell or insure houses, you are in "the service sector."

If you are making cars, you're in the "goods-producing sector;" if you're driving a cab, you're in services.

Some economists lump government in with services, but many make a distinction between "the public sector," which includes government and nonprofit organizations, and "the private sector," which is divided, as mentioned above, into goods and services.

The services area may be growing faster than goods, but there are plenty of service jobs that are being automated: cashiers are being replaced by ATMs, which work twenty-four hours a day, seven days a week, with no coffee breaks. Retail clerks are losing jobs as more people shop electronically. Even musicians are losing jobs—as a single keyboard player can make the sounds of several instruments.

SELL, SELL, SELL

You're tired of being poor. You want a lifestyle, now. You can handle rejection. You'll do anything. You are ready for sales.

The good thing about selling is that if you can stand it, and you're any good, you will never have to worry about finding a job. Just walk up to a sales manager and say, "I don't need a salary; just give me business cards and put me on commission." They'll hire you (at a lower starter commission level)—what have they got to lose?

48 🦉 Stockbroker

Fred is taking the fastest route he could find to financial stability. He's working as a stockbroker.

"I don't understand all of my classmates who are acting like they're still in college. I'm out. I'm glad I'm out. And the last thing I want to do is go back. I went to college so I could get a good job, and I've got one. This may seem unfashionable, but I had the experience of working for my uncle in his plumbing business to pay him for money he put toward my college tuition, and that showed me what I don't want to do.

"Sure, I have to dress respectably. But that's no big deal. I work hard during the day, but my day ends early. I'm rarely in the office past 5 P.M. And I don't take work home or worry about it on the weekends. Being in sales, I get rejected now and again, but who doesn't?

"Yes, I'm in sales. A lot of my colleagues deny that. They say that they're consultants. But anytime a lot of your income comes from commissions, you're in sales, and you might as well admit it.

"I work for a top firm. The people who sell well, do well. And I'm starting to trade my own portfolio as well. I don't have enough clients yet, but I'm getting there. If you have the guts for it, this is the greatest game in town, and you don't need an MBA to play."

How did you get the job?

"I went through the college alumni directory and called every alum at a top brokerage house and asked for advice. The guy here was so happy to meet a kid who wanted to get to work and sell that he promised me a job on the spot. I doubt he was authorized to do that, but he produces enough to have the juice to make it happen."

Checking Out a Company

Before you apply for work at a company, it's worth getting to know as much about it as you can. Here are just a few of the things you can do:

- Talk to everyone you know who works there. Ask them what the company is really like. If you don't know anyone who works there, call your college's job placement (career counseling) alumni office and see if they can give you a name and number.
- Get a copy of the company's annual report before you have your first interview, so you have enough information to ask intelligent questions about the company. Ways to get annual reports include requesting them from stockbrokers or calling a company's main number and asking to speak to the Investor Relations Department. Annual reports are also often there for the taking in the reception area at a company's headquarters.
- If you know a stockbroker, ask if they have any analyst's reports on the company or industry.
- If you have access to an electronic data source like Nexis or Lexis, search the recent articles on the company. Your friends who are still in school may be able to help you with this.
- Find a copy of *The 100 Best Companies to Work for in America*, by Robert Levering and Milton Moskowitz. Get the latest issue you can find. The paperback version is published by Plume. If the company's mentioned in there, you'll get a good picture of its corporate culture.
- Call the local Better Business Bureau and see if they have anything to say about the company.
- If you are worried about karmic issues, there are ways to check out a company's performance on all sorts of issues, including environmental, racial, gender, sexual preference, union, involvement in military areas, exploitation of third-world labor, etc.
- If the company in question makes consumer goods, look

them up in *Shopping for a Better World,* a book put out by the Council on Economic Priorities. Also, find the most recent copy of "Boycott Action News," published in *Co-op America Quarterly.* (If you can't find this publication, contact Co-op America, 1612 K Street NW, #600, Washington, DC 20006, (202) 872-5307.)

• For large companies without consumer products, you can look to see if a company's stock is in the portfolios of the "ethical" mutual finds like Calvert, Parnassus, or Working Assets. (Call the fund and ask for its most recent portfolio listing.)

49 🦉 Travel Agent

Fern is a travel agent. Her coworkers would object to her calling it selling: they think of themselves as consultants (just like the stockbrokers). But, to Fern, it's selling.

"I'm still enjoying this because I'm still learning. The main way I'm learning is by taking 'fam trips,' trips provided for free to travel agents so we can get firsthand knowledge of facilities. A lot of the other agents here don't travel anymore. They can't give a firsthand account of most of the places they send people—they read them info from ads and brochures.

"I like to send people to places where I can tell them which side of the hotel is quietest, tell them if the bartender is friendly, and tell them if the carpet stinks. And I check in with my customers after they get back. I can't believe the other agents don't do that. It's great information.

"I have to work harder because I'm newer. The older agents have steady customers who fly first class, who book for their whole business, and all of that. But I'll catch up in no time. I'm making myself the company expert in adventure travel. I know all about rafting trips all over the world, and if you want to go llama trekking, I'm the one to talk to."

"My mother has worked here for years. My coming aboard meant she could cut back on her hours. I did all the basic training years ago so I could work here during the summers, so reading the Official Airline Guide and using the Sabre reservations system are nothing new to me."

Employment at Will

"Employment at will" means you don't have a contract.

Theoretically speaking it might be better for you to have your rights spelled out in a specific performance contract or a collective bargaining agreement. But the odds are you won't be offered a contract, so "employment at will" is the unwritten contract that sets up the basic terms. You work as long as both you and the company are happy with the arrangement. You can leave when you want, and you can be fired without cause. It's what you'll be offered in most cases.

Under "employment at will" you are protected by the state wage and hours laws that determine the minimum wage and how long the company can wait before giving you your check.

In some cases, employment at will will be better than having a contract. If you are asked to sign a contract with a "non-compete" clause in it that requires you not to work in the industry you're in for a period of time after leaving the company, think hard before signing. Although those clauses are often not enforceable in court, they might make a potential new employer hesitate to hire you. It's not necessarily a good idea to give your boss the ability to say that either you work for them or you don't work at all.

Being an "employee at will" is, of course, much better

50 🦉 Insurance Salesperson

Paul sells insurance—and likes it.

"I had this horrible image of insurance sales, until I met Gianni. He really is serious about being a consultant, not a salesperson. He won't sell you something if he doesn't think it's right for you. He really does want you to be his customer for life.

"He didn't sell me a policy—I have no money. But he did sell me a job. He's what I was looking for: a mentor, a model. I learned how to sell by watching him. He's a master."

"It's taken me a while to get licensed, but now I have a financial plan that will let me retire at fifty. The great thing about insurance is the payments you get when your customers renew. I know that if I work hard now, things will be easier later.

"This is what I needed. A professional job that I could start right away, where the harder I work, the more I make. I've still got a lot to learn, but I also have a lot to earn. That's what happens when you start a family early.

"The family perspective helps me sell. Before I had obligations, I couldn't really see the need for a lot of insurance. Now I really see how it helps provide families with the security and flexibility they need."

How did you get the job?

"Gianni runs informational seminars on being in the business. I saw a flyer for one on a bulletin board at college."

Go Ahead, Brag

As a job seeker, you need to get used to presenting your work and life experience in a positive light. There's a fine line here. There's no point in going around sounding like an idiot—if your friends know that you're a dog walker, there's no point in insisting that they all refer to you as an "expert facilitator of non-human companion health-enhancing activities." At the same time, if you walk six different dogs a day and have successfully hired substitutes when you have been unavailable, you have every right to talk about what you do as managing an entrepreneurial business.

You can try to practice on your parents, if you still have parents and can still talk to them easily. They are often worse than prospective employers. To at least some prospective employers, you are a potential adult employee—to your parents, you are always a child.

You can try and practice on your friends, but they might crack up and make you self-conscious. But keep practicing. What you do for work is a serious issue, no matter what your friends think. And if you aren't willing to be a cheerleader and number-one fan for yourself, who else will be? (OK, your dog. But that won't help in the job search.)

Rudy is a master at being upbeat about himself and about his work history. Ask him about his first job and he'll tell you it was his paper route. Don't laugh. It counts. And when he answers that way he's showing the kind of thinking that he needs to show in order to get work these days. It *was* a job. It shows that he had initiative, that he's learned something about reliability, that he can make change, and that he's already learned that customer satisfaction counts.

For that matter, he could have cited his experience as a choirboy as his first job. It doesn't sound like much of a job at first, but when you start thinking that there were rehearsals three days a week as well as services on Sunday, that promptness was essential, as were good behavior, ties, and shined shoes, it begins to sound much more like a job.

And when you add the fact that he was promoted to choir librarian, which required extra time correctly collating sheet music and placing it in the choir stalls before the service, and collecting and filing it afterward, he starts to sound like a model, ambitious employee. When you add in the fact that he was eventually promoted to crucifer, the one who leads the whole choir procession, it becomes clear that he has distinct leadership potential and is destined for management.

51   Media Salesperson

Monica is a "space cadet." In other words, she sells advertising space for a magazine.

"Last summer I was an intern in an ad agency. Every two weeks, I was moved into another department. While I was in the Media Department, a media buyer took me along on four of her business luncheons. She was so poor that she relied on these luncheons for half of her diet. I decided right then and there that I didn't want to be the starving media buyer, I wanted to be the media sales rep with an expense account.

"My first thought was that I'd work for *Cosmo* or *Time* or *Vanity Fair* or *Bride's* or something like that. Dream on. Those places don't hire you until you've had experience. But the more I researched it, the more magazines I found. Every profession has a couple of books, meaning magazines, that sell to it. And, surprisingly, they're not all headquartered in New York or Los Angeles.

"Interviewing is important to become a rep. The companies have to know that you are presentable and can think on your feet. I admitted that I didn't have a perfect command of all the technical terms and issues, like 'controlled circulations' and 'ABC statements.' But I also made a convincing case for the magazine on the basis of its unique features and its authority with readers.

"I think another reason I got hired was that they knew that their New York rep didn't always do well with the young media buyers, but they couldn't get rid of him because a lot of old clients had known him for years. Now I'm his assistant. For the first month, we made all our calls together, which he hated, I could tell. He had to watch what he said, forget the nasty jokes, and keep his drinking down. Now that I know the ropes, we break things up this way: he calls on the old boozers; I call on everyone else.

"He's always after me to get my expense account numbers up so he won't look bad. His average lunch appointment includes several drinks and steaks at a stuffy place, while my average client might have one wine spritzer, and he spends a ton taking people to sports events. I've developed my own style. I take my clients for facials and pedicures—it's a real treat and we get to stay on our diets."

How did you get the job?

"I went back to the Media Department at the agency where I had been an intern, and used their files. They had cabinets full of media kits. I'd study up on the kit, and on the competitive reports the agency had prepared, call the publisher, and go talk. When I was hired, my publisher told me a big part of my job was to stay on good terms with the agency where I had temped. Being introduced, in effect, by a big customer, counts."

You Don't Start in Management

Even if Mummy and Daddy started the firm, the odds are you are going to have to start your working life somewhere down the food chain from the executive suite. (Of course if they did start the firm, you won't stay down there long.) It's a little like high school: you don't start as a senior. You start as a peon, and work up as new peons come along.

Some people think that a diploma is like a Monopoly card that says "Pass Go, Collect $200." It's not. You still have to start at the beginning and collect a few war stories before you get to the boardroom.

This may seem like an annoyance, but it's sensible. Companies can't be run on theory alone. Management has to know something about how things work in the real world, how the sales process works and what customers really care about. Think of your entry-level job as a chance to learn, and as a challenge—to get promoted.

52 🦉 Printer's Rep

Claude sells financial printing services.

"Financial printing is an area I knew nothing about while in college, but it's a big industry. Every publicly owned company prints annual reports and 10-K forms, and every initial public offering creates a blizzard of printed paper. And lawyers and investment bankers don't come to the printers; the printers send salespeople to them.

"These folks don't kid around. A whole class of us were trained together in the midwest. Full days of training in business terms and practices, sales techniques, and printing. Even if you're the most junior member of your team, you know your stuff.

"The expectations are high. I have to make several calls a day, and these are people who are hard to get in to see and who are notorious for canceling. Time that they can't bill for is low on their priorities. If I don't look good and do well, I won't last here. But I will."

How did you get the job?

"When I was looking into jobs, I met with an investment banker. He asked me why I wanted to be an investment banker. I told him, 'to get rich.' He told me that if I wanted to get rich, I should sell financial printing. He had just found out that his financial printing rep owned a plane. I asked him for some names. Then I went through a lot of aptitude testing and interviewing and applications. As I said, these folks don't fool around."

Schooling Never Stops

The old idea that "all the schooling you need happens early in your life and then all the working happens" is dead wrong. Schooling now happens repeatedly throughout adult life as you are trained to take on new challenges.

This is bad news for you if you hated school, but it's reality. The world is moving so fast that few of us will have the luxury of learning just one thing and sticking to it.

What will you be learning? Here are just a few of the possibilities:

- How to operate a new piece of equipment
- How to use the company's new E-mail system
- How to "prospect" for new customers
- How to handle yourself in a public relations emergency ("media-training")
- How to use direct mail to promote your company
- What questions you are allowed to ask when hiring a potential employee, and which are illegal
- How to be a better member of a team
- How to be a better leader
- How to do "consultative selling"
- How to appreciate and promote diversity
- How to focus on quality
- How to determine what type of person you're dealing with and how to use that knowledge to communicate better
- How to manage your time
- How to think more creatively
- How to write more clearly

How to Make Use of a Useless Degree

- How to measure your department's progress through "benchmarking"
- What your rights are under a workers' compensation system.

Some of what you'll learn is hard and factual; some will be softer and more "touchy-feely." And, even the people who hated school sometimes like business-related education. The payoff for this kind of education can be a lot more direct, and a lot more tangible.

53 🦉 Telemarketer

Stanley is a TSR— a telephone sales representative. He works in a "boiler room," a room full of desks and phones. He's probably calling you right now to try and sell you a subscription to a book club.

"This is the pits. The worst. But that's what makes it good for me. I don't believe in the people I work for; I don't owe them anything. They get me for the hours I'm there, and that's all. I bring no problems home; they are no part of my identity. And I won't get caught doing it forever. I'll definitely move on.

"Here's the deal. They give me a script to follow, and the numbers are automatically dialed. I could do better if I ad-libbed, but they do random monitoring of the calls we make, so I stick to the script. I get rejected a lot, and I move on. I am ruthless about getting off of calls with people who don't hear well, or who sound too lonely—they take too long. I'm not here to play Miss Lonelyhearts—I'm working for dough.

"Even though I have the worst attitude, I win a lot of the cash awards they give to keep us motivated: most-sales-this-hour-wins-$50-cash kind of things. My English is a lot better than the English of a lot of the people here in purgatory, and that helps.

"On top of that, the people I sell seem to stay sold. I lose very few calls in the verification stage. I think that's because I don't sell hard, I only sell the people who sound like they want to be sold."

How did you get the job?

"Simple, I answered an ad in the paper."

The Postmodern Dilemma

At the rate that productivity is growing, pretty soon, a small percentage of the population will be able to produce all of the goods that the rest of us will need. In theory, there won't be enough work to go around, and a number of us will be free to devote our time to art and leisure activities. Sounds pretty good. And in a system where no matter how hard you work you will lose your job at some point, and have to change careers occasionally, volunteering to skip the job part and go straight to the leisure and arts gig sounds like a sane response.

The problem is that the system is set up to give the rewards of greater productivity to those who are still working, and to "owners" whose capital is working for them. In other words, you still need a job to pay the rent. And the only way most of us will have the money for long vacations is if we're working too hard to be able to take them.

54 🦉 Selling Real Estate

Phil sells real estate. He makes his own hours and gets to stay strongly involved with the community he lives in.

"The first step was getting a license. It was a hassle, but not hard. I took a cram course and went for the test while my college-honed test-taking skills were still there. I already had an agreement with the broker.

"I think of it as running a dating service for houses and people. I never really feel like I'm selling—just matching up. The great thing about real estate is you're selling something tangible, something people can see, touch and feel.

"I also think of it as educating. When I get a prospect who isn't ready to buy, I still take them through all of the forms so they'll be ready when the time comes. I drive them by a few houses to give them an idea of what places are going for, and I explain basic things like how mortgages work and what home inspectors do. People really appreciate all that. I sell them when they're ready, and meanwhile I get a lot of referrals.

"If you're halfway ambitious, you can make good money really quickly. Figure what the average house in your neighborhood sells for. Every time I'm part of a deal, I get 1 or 1½ percent of that. If I put through a deal a month, I make good money.

"I know some people who like the big real estate franchise operations like Century 21 or ERA, but they're not for me. I specialize in knowing this city, and this area, not in being a part of a chain of trained automatons in matching polyester jackets. I was with an office when they joined a chain and they started having us watch training films with lines like 'Is this the two-bedroom model or the three?' The only problem is, this is a northeastern city, not a new California development. We don't have 'models;' everything is different.

"Plus I'm really not comfortable with all of the sales manipulation techniques. I appreciate the importance of 'qualifying' people—checking out their financial backgrounds to make sure they can really afford a house—that's part of our job. But all of the closes they teach you, to try and get people to make up their minds on the spot, aren't for me. Buying a house is a big decision. It's OK by me if you need a little time.

"The biggest hassle is that to do this job right, you need to give up your weekends. That's when people are available to see houses. It really messes up your social life. The good thing, however, is that they don't expect you to hang around the office. If you hang around, they say you're not doing your job."

How did you get the job?

"I saw an ad in the paper and went in to talk to them. I would have had to have three eyes not to get the job. Realistically, what do they have to lose? They pay on commission. All they risk is a little training time and some desk and phone space."

Being an "Independent Contractor"

Phil is an independent contractor. An independent contractor is paid to do a task, but they're not on the payroll. They generally submit invoices reflecting an agreed hourly, daily, weekly, or monthly rate, an agreed project rate, or an agreed per piece rate. They are supposed to have the freedom to set their own hours and work conditions. Many independent contractors use their own equipment; a number work from home.

Many companies like to use independent contractors because that means they don't have to pay benefits and withhold taxes. When you're an employee, you cost the company a whole lot more than just your salary. They may end up paying health benefits, a retirement fund, a profit sharing fund, vacation days, sick days, maternity leave. If you are injured, they may have to pay for your rehabilitation; if you are fired, they may have to pay toward your unemployment benefits.

It's a reasonable deal: the independent contractor gets freedom; the company has fewer costs. But some companies take advantage of the situation by treating people like employees, while paying them as independent contractors. The tax authorities have been cracking down on this recently.

If you are told when to work, where to be, how to do it,

and what to wear, you probably should be paid as an employee. Learn your benefits and take advantage of them.

If you are an independent contractor, exercise your greater freedoms, and remember that you are responsible for your own health care insurance and your own retirement, so you should be making more than employees doing the same work.

If you get a job as an independent contractor, the first thing you should do is figure out how to file estimated taxes and make payments quarterly. The easy way is to have an accountant do this, but the forms are allegedly simple enough for any of us to figure out. If you don't do this, your second year as an independent contractor will be miserable, because you'll be working to pay two years' taxes and aren't likely to have much. It's tough to put aside money for taxes when you are just starting out, but you have to do it.

MANAGE

If you think about it, you probably have some experience that could be called managing: keeping track of the dues for your scout troop, coordinating volunteers for Earth Day, being captain of your soccer team, creating the chore list and rotation for your group house.

Keeping track of things, keeping them going, keeping them documented are all skills that you may already have, and that you probably can develop.

Here's how five people are managing.

55   Property Manager

Property doesn't just take care of itself, and a lot of owners have so much property that they hire management companies who assign people to manage their properties. That's what Sean does.

"There are all sorts of levels to property management. A lot of janitors and superintendents call themselves property managers, but that's not what I'm talking about. I have overall responsibility for the physical plant and for the fiscal health of the buildings I'm assigned to. I can tell you what the bylaws of the co-ops are, who the lawyers and accountants are, what their arrears look like, and where they are in every lawsuit and renovation. And, unfortunately, every building has at least one pain-in-the-ass troublemaker, and I know all of their voices by heart.

"It helps that I have an engineering background. I have basic understanding of HVAC systems—that's heating, ventilation, and air conditioning. I don't think you should manage a building without knowing this.

"I keep meticulous records and files on my buildings. There has historically been a lot of bribery and kickbacks between contractors and building managers, and people are starting to do a lot of investigating. I want to be able to document that everything I do is aboveboard.

"It's an odd mix of business and nonbusiness. Co-op boards can be amazingly petty. And sometimes people fall behind on their rent and call me up. They don't understand that I act for the owners, but I am not an owner. It's not my job to bend the rules; I don't have that authority. I don't like that sort of situation. But, for the most part, this is a great job."

"I looked in the newspaper for a listing for people with HVAC knowledge."

Catch-22

You need experience to get a job, but you need a job to get experience.

It used to be that there was such a thing as a starter job in almost every area. New recruits joined a company and were "shown the ropes."

Now, as one recruiter said, "There's no such thing as unskilled or inexperienced anymore. Everybody wants to hire people who are experienced in their exact business. No one wants to train."

The Experience Catch-22 is what's driving so many people to take internships. It's a way of getting experience. People are also getting experience through temp jobs. And, on occasion, people are lying about their experience in order to get jobs.

One actor we talked to said that he would claim anything to be able to get an acting job, and then go learn it. He once learned fencing in a weekend, and once spent a week training to look like a professional driver. He did get caught once. He was in a commercial where he and an actress were supposed to drive off into the sunset in a convertible; but he didn't know how to drive a standard transmission. The director went nuts, but they eventually hid someone at his feet who worked the clutch with his hands, and the camera angle was changed to show the actors from the shoulders up.

When you're asked an "experience" question, try to think of something similar that you know how to do. If you say "I've never used Paradox, but I've used Excel, another database program, so I'm sure I could pick it up quickly," you put yourself way ahead of all the candidates who just say no.

56 🦉 Account Executive

Advertising has a reputation as a young person's business, so it's not a bad place for a young job hunter to look. Grant is a "suit;" he works on the management side, as opposed to the "creative" side.

"Advertising has a reputation of being a glamorous business, but lots of agencies take advantage of the fact that people want to be in the ad business to get people to work for peanuts or work gruelingly long days. I think the glory days are long passed.

"Much of my job is documentation. If we have a meeting, or even if I just have a phone call with a client, I write a call report and distribute it to everyone involved with the account. If I need some creative or research done, I write a briefing, and open up a job requisition. If I want to add or change information to a work in progress, I issue a 'buck slip.' Meanwhile, I issue account status reports which go to everyone and their brothers.

"A big part of what I do is fight for internal resources. This place is ridiculously short-staffed, and a bit top-heavy. We're always hiring people whose job it is to delegate and think and comment. They criticize and develop new strategies and positions. But they don't get things done. So I have to run around begging the few people who actually work to pay attention to my accounts.

"The only time when I feel like I have any clout is when I meet with the media reps. They will do what I say faster than my own people, so I use them for a lot of research. I also do a better job than our media department of getting merchandising (concessions, giveaways, freebies) out of them."

How did you get the job?

"I started out in the Traffic Department of a small agency. My job was to carry print ads around the agency, getting all of the people involved to approve and sign the ad at each stage of its production. It was a great way to get to know the business and to get noticed. One of the account managers noticed me and I became a part of the account team, an assistant account executive. That essentially translates as 'errand boy.' I love the team, but I'm starting to burn out. I work eleven-hour days, five days a week, and often on weekends. I just am not enough of a samurai to keep it up."

Yes, Some People Do Value a Liberal Arts Background

If you studied liberal arts in college, don't despair. Several of the Human Resource people we spoke to respect and value liberal arts backgrounds.

One said, "At the ad agency, we were looking for people who could sit in a room and keep up with the client as the conversation changed direction at a hundred miles an hour. That meant we needed someone with an open mind and a broad background. Every time I hired anyone who was an advertising major, it caused trouble. They came in thinking they knew all the answers and we had to deprogram them before we could retrain them."

Another said, "A business major who comes in thinking they understand business is trouble from the start. I don't care if they understand theory. I want to know if they're smart enough to realize that a twenty-five-year-old pipsqueak has no place telling a fifty-year-old self-made multimillionaire that he's doing everything all wrong. Give me a history major any day. They come in humble, they listen, and they generally are smart enough to come back and ask for advice before making pronouncements."

How to Make Use of a Useless Degree

57 🦉 Retail

Alyssa read a book about Sam Walton, the founder of Wal-Mart, and decided that retail was the only business to be in.

"Retailing is going to remain important, no matter where the economy goes. Even if more goods are sold electronically, that's still retailing, and there's going to be a big demand for people who understand retail management practices like pricing, merchandising, and inventory.

"People think that just because they've been shopping, they know how retail works. There's a lot more to it than standing in the front of the store and saying, 'Good morning, Mrs. Jones' to a regular customer. If you don't understand inventory, for example, the inventory carrying costs will eat you alive, and 'shrinkage'—theft by employees—will ruin you. We learn a lot from regional executives, and a lot from our peers. I always come away from a meeting with a lot of new ideas.

"Woolworth, the company I work for, is a lot more diverse than you would think. They have specialty chains, sports chains, and discount chains, as well as the old five-and-dime chain, which, incidentally, has some of the most valuable real estate contracts in the world.

"A lot of what I'm learning has to do with dealing with people. Managing people and customers is a big part of retail management. Recently, I caught a shoplifter, and I got in trouble. I saw her taking the stuff and had some of the female employees take her into a dressing room and have her remove her shirt, which was where she was hiding the watches. But I got in trouble because that wasn't the procedure. The store got sued. In other words, this is more complicated than you would think."

"I went around to all the stores where I normally shop and asked to speak to the managers. I asked them about their companies' training programs. The people at the Woolworth chain seemed pretty psyched, so I sent them an inquiry letter."

Go into the Family Business

Going into the family business is an option for more people than you would think. Some estimates are that 90 percent of the companies in the U.S. are family run or family controlled. There are a lot of good arguments for going into a family firm, if your family has one, not the least of which is that you will probably have a chance to get a greater equity share than you would in any other situation. There are also good arguments against it. Families and business don't always mix well, and family conflicts can get magnified when the stakes are raised. The Binghams and the Hafts are just two of the many business-owning families who have had bitter public feuds.

Abe works in the family firm with his father. Allie works with her father and brothers. And Elaine works in her family's business. But none of them went straight from school into the family firm; each spent a few years working for other companies, so they joined the family firm having proven themselves in the open market.

Allie made it a point to learn research, marketing, and advertising, so she could bring new expertise to a family firm that already had plenty of experts in manufacturing.

At first, Elaine had no intention of joining the family firm. Her family was competitive enough without their all being in business together. But after a few years working for other people, she realized that she wanted to work for an aggressive firm where her natural competitiveness would be valued, and the family company began to look pretty good.

All three are happy they are in the family business. But all are happy they didn't go straight there.

If you are thinking of going into a family business, it's worth reading *Mind Your Own Business* by Marcy Syms, the president and C.O.O. of Syms. (You can order it for $18.95 plus $2.00 postage and handling from MasterMedia Limited, 17 E. 89th Street, New York, NY 10128, (212) 260-5600 or (800) 334-8232 or (fax) (212) 546-7607.) Marcy Syms knows the topic from the inside: she went into her family's business. She's also surveyed a number of other people in successful family businesses. Her book will alert you to a lot of things to think about and look out for before you make your decision.

58 Management Consultant

Charles is a management consultant. He speaks about "best practices," "work planning," "managing deliverables," and "benchmarking."

"Andersen Consulting brings in a lot of twenty-two year olds straight from college, with no business experience. They refer to us as 'green beans.' Green beans are sent to Andersen's three-week training boot camp at our Center for Professional Education in St. Charles, Illinois. It's mind-numbing; you can't learn it all, but at least you get familiar with the terms and concepts.

"How can a twenty-something right out of college have any credibility with older, experienced corporate managers? You have to leverage the firm's experience. All the resources are there—you just have to take the initiative to find them. From that angle, it's sink or swim. You also have to learn by watching. I learned a lot about meeting facilitation by attending meetings run by our senior people.

"I think the company has a really healthy culture. Since

what we sell is our people, there's a strong emphasis on developing and protecting your people—it's an important criteria."

How did you get the job?

"Andersen recruits on campus. I had to pass a lot of tests, and interview with a lot of people at different levels, but they basically came to me."

First Day at an Office Job

Your first day at a new company can be one of the best. Enjoy it. You probably get to park in the convenient visitor's parking lot and might even get taken out for lunch or drinks.

Here are some things you should do before they start piling the work on:

- Find out where the bathrooms are and whether you need a key.
- Find out when people in your department really get in.
- Meet the security guard and make friends. You may misplace your I.D. tag some day. Get the I.D., keys, or magnetic card you need for access. Find out when the building is closed and how you can get in on weekends.
- Meet the phone operator, learn how the phone system works and what your number is.
- Learn the receptionist's name.
- Find the supply closet.
- Throw out all the catsup packets your predecessor left in the desk.
- Find out if there's a coffee machine and how it works (even if you don't drink coffee).
- Find out the copier rules: Do you have to sign for copies? Do you change toner, or is that someone's job?
- If you have a computer, change the access code. Use a keyword that you will remember.

How to Make Use of a Useless Degree

- If the company has E-mail, read a bunch of it first before you start posting, so you know the local etiquette.
- Don't swear until someone else does.
- Find out the parking space pecking order.
- Don't ask where the petty cash is kept and who's in charge (that sounds suspicious), but keep your ears open for this information.
- If you have a cubicle, put up one personal picture.
- Find out what your predecessor did wrong and don't repeat it.
- Find out when the messengers and air couriers pick up.
- Start making a glossary of all the abbreviations and acronyms the people in the office use.
- Make sure Personnel has seen your passport and whatever proof they need that you're a citizen.
- Have someone in your department call the Payroll/Accounting folks. Make sure Accounting has your social security number and number of deductions, and knows whether you want direct deposit or not so they can get you entered into the system for the next paycheck cycle. (Many companies use an outside payroll service to issue paychecks. If you go to Accounting the day before your check is due, they often can't cut you a paycheck, even if they want to.) Few things are more demoralizing than to start a new job and have to beg and borrow money for a whole month just to cover commuting and food. If the people in Accounting want to see you, visit them immediately. Be very nice to these people. The odds are good that they will be processing your expense checks, too.

---

59 🦉 Special Events Coordinator

Imagine getting paid to run parties. Now stop imagining, because it's nowhere near as much fun as it sounds. But it is a real job—and, in every city there are people, like P.Z., who are getting paid to put on special events.

"One of the best things about event planning is that you get to work with a lot of good causes. Museums, schools, and hospitals all use special events as a major part of their development—development being a fancy word for fund-raising.

"Each project lasts from six months to a year. The fund-raising ones last longer because there is a lot involved in choosing the right event and the right chairman and cochairman, and honorees, and following up on all the lists to make sure people are coming or making a donation.

"Corporate events don't include all that solicitation, but there's still a lot to them. The planning is intense. Booking the place, planning the menus, the seating, the place cards, the band, the flowers. When the event finally happens, you're there for setup, you greet the guests, and you hang in there long after it's over, making sure everything is cleaned up and the people at the facility get their tips.

"You're not going to get rich doing this. I felt like a queen when I got bumped up from $7 an hour to $14. But I like it. And if I ever want to go into another business I'm sure meeting the right people.

"It sounds weird, but the best test for whether you'd be good at this business is whether you're good at throwing parties in your regular life. In college, I was the only one I knew who threw dinner parties. I'm a natural. I like worrying about the guest list and who sits where and what the flowers will look like. I enjoy it, but I never relax at a party. Everyone thinks it comes so easily to me. It doesn't. Parties work when you work at making them work."

How did you get the job?

"Through the girl grapevine. Two of my friends were working an event and they brought me on board. It turned out that I knew more about food service, having grown up in the restaurant business, so I am pretty valuable to them."

Job Hunting Expenses

Keep close track of all your job hunting expenses: if you get that big, high-paying job, some of these expenses may be deductible. (Yes—that was an incredibly wishy-washy statement. But we are not tax experts, and, as you'd expect, the law isn't something simple like "All job hunting expenses are deductible," and if it were, we wouldn't trust the Internal Revenue people to *keep* it simple.)

Record all the expenses, including the cost of this book, the cost of having your resumé designed, the cost of traveling to other areas to look for work, the phone and postage costs, and anything else you can think of. Then check with an accountant or read the small print for the year you're filing.

CREATE!
PERFORM!

Have you ever noticed how radiant actors look when they're talking about "their craft"? Part of it is professional makeup, great lighting, and being trained to look good on camera. But another part of it is that many people, particularly the ones who think of themselves as creative, are happiest when they are creating.

Here are six people whose jobs directly involve their creative abilities.

60 🦉 Art Director

Art directors are designers. They are responsible for the look of ads, movie scenes, bank forms, and other visual communications. Jolene is an assistant art director at a packaging design firm.

"One of my big problems in life is figuring out how to tell my family what it is that I do. I design packaging, but I don't take the pictures, I don't draw the art—I decide what picture should be taken, or what art created, and I hire the artist who does it, although actually we have an art buyer who does that.

"A lot of what I do involves knowing how colors shift when photos are taken. If you photograph a box of cereal or a can of soda, the picture looks different from the way it looks in real life. So I create a lot of fake packaging with colors that aren't the real ones, but photograph like the real ones.

"A lot of what I do has to do with a sense of type. People don't realize how important type is—to me, the shape and spacing of the letters is as important a communication as the words. More important, in fact, because the reader isn't aware of it."

How did you get the job?

"I studied design, and my senior year I won a competition for the most innovative packaging design. I made extra copies of my prototype and sent them to design firms I wanted to work for. They like to hire people who appreciate the challenges of packaging. Most design students want to go into advertising or the movies."

Moving to Get Away from Your Parents

Jason got out of college and found an entry-level job in advertising. His father didn't think the job or the pay was enough, so he sent Jason to a Dale Carnegie course. While there's nothing wrong with going to a Dale Carnegie course—lots of people find it gives them more confidence, and ongoing education is smart, and college certainly didn't prepare Jason for the work world—the fact still remained that Jason was sent; he didn't choose to go.

He realized that he'd never be in charge of his own career as long as he was on the East Coast. So he moved to California, where he is doing just fine. In fact, he's confident that, in a couple of years, he could move back if he wanted to, and have relatively little trouble dealing with his parents.

"I thought I had established my independence in college. But I guess I hadn't. My tuition was still being paid for, and a lot of decisions were being made for me. It sounds like I ran away from a problem, but I make no apologies for it. I did what I needed to do."

61 🦉 On-line Service Content Provider

Brando's receiving, as he says, "significant cash flow" from providing information and inspirational messages and exercises about child abuse on an on-line forum. He is creating something he fervently believes in, and it's supporting him.

"The hunger, the need, for information about abuse and recovery out there is vaster than you can imagine. And I have a way of providing this healing perspective that's more anonymous, more immediate, and more interactive than the recovery books in bookstores.

"I get paid based on the amount of activity my forum generates. You'd be amazed at the activity reports. The average person stays for hours. And the messages they post would break your heart.

"It wasn't easy to master the tools needed to create and run this forum, but it's been worth it. And the job has gotten so big that I now hire nine others, and need more. We have touched and helped, and been helped ourselves, by tens of thousands of people who would be embarrassed to get a mailing or buy a book but, in the darkness and loneliness of the night, find their way to our forum, discover that they are not alone, and are helped along the road to recovery. There are people who were ready to kill themselves before they found us—we're making a difference."

How did you get the job?

"The job found me. I was lost. I had no real calling. But then I had a breakthrough private on-line chat about abuse. I typed things I'd never said, and my doing that helped someone I've never seen and whose real name I'll never know. And I knew at that moment that this was what I needed to be doing."

Content Will Rule

Lots of people are talking and writing about the Internet, but not enough of them are pointing out that the Internet, and other media, will create an increased need for "content." Sure, you could get a job installing the fiber-optic cable of the Internet; but you can also find a future spot for yourself by providing information, entertainment, or a perspective that's valuable to a particular audience.

The truly valuable person will be the one who has a unique point of view. What this person says or does is what will get people to *use* the Internet—instead of just talking about it.

If Herb trips, he instinctively curls around his camera as he falls. He doesn't care if he gets hurt; he's protecting his camera. He's a photographer.

"I knew I wanted to make a living taking pictures, but I didn't know how to pull it off. I did some PR photography, but it was completely artless. Go to a real estate association awards banquet. Use a flash gun on everyone who wins an award. Supply contact sheets, and then fulfill orders of 8 x 10 glossies for local papers and office decor. But it paid for a lot of equipment.

"For the moment, my rule is, I don't shoot people. I shoot nature and city shots that are sold at crafts fairs and I also do architectural shots for real estate companies and architects—that calls for special equipment, and real patience about natural light.

"Of course, I also take a lot of pictures for myself: my work, my art. I'd like someday to be recognized as a photographer, to have an exhibit or two and maybe do a book."

How did you get the job?

"My grandmother gave me a Brownie camera when I was eleven. If there ever was a question of doing anything else, it was solved the first time I went into a darkroom and printed one of my own shots. It's a magical experience. It's like alchemy."

Barbie Had Lots of Careers

Getting grief about how many different kinds of work you've tried? If you had a Barbie doll when you were little, tell whoever's bugging you that Barbie is your role model, and she had lots of careers: stewardess, model, actress, etc.

Or if someone is giving you grief about switching careers, and he or she happens to be divorced, reply that lifelong careers and lifelong marriages are both great concepts— but they don't appear to be the dominant models in today's world.

63   Musician

Ken is a trained, serious musician. For a while he tried to get by getting commissions, but he just couldn't make enough money. He's still composing serious music, but he also plays keyboard and synthesizer in a band that gets paid.

"We play favorites and oldies in Atlantic City casinos. Every now and then I slip in a little Erik Satie or even Mozart, just to see if anyone notices. It's not my life's ambition to play 'Celebrate' twice a night, but its work. We also play parties.

"It's hard to imagine being a musician and being a 'normal' person. It just doesn't work that way. We, literally, march to a different drummer. A lot of what other people do through talking I do through music. Communicating, expressing. It is a gift, but a demanding one. No matter what kind of job I had, I'd still be playing at midnight, so I might as well make that my job.

"If it weren't for the ocean, this would be the most depressing place on earth. It's not really my kind of music, but it's music. It gets through. And, in its way, it's the right music for this place. We're thinking of cutting a CD of music to gamble by. Why not?"

How did you get the job?

"I first played in the band when they were going through a pretentious phase and wanted someone who could give them a portentous, symphonic sound on a synthesizer. They came to the college looking for music majors, and I looked the least geeky."

One Job Might Not Be Enough

Finding and keeping one job is going to be tough enough. But it gets worse—you may need to have more than one at the same time.

Lots of jobs are only part-time—companies like that because they don't generally pay part-timers benefits. And many part-time jobs don't pay enough to support the lifestyle that a lot of people aspire to. Because of these drawbacks, and because of all the extra commuting involved, two half-time jobs don't add up to a full-time job: they add up to less than full-time pay and benefits for more than full-time hassles.

The upside of having two jobs is that it's not likely that you'll lose both of them at the same time. You have a little more security and you're getting experience in two different places, and perhaps two different skills, at the same time.

64 🦉 Actor

Ned is a dedicated actor, which, in New York, would normally mean that he's a waiter. But he's not.

"I don't recommend waiting for actors. It gets in the way of two many auditions, and it somehow makes you subservient, has too much stress, and robs you of the poise you need for auditions. I work the graveyard shift, from midnight to 8 A.M., at a hotel desk. I can read, write, and do research whenever it's quiet, and I have my days free. I can sleep right up to an audition and go in with lots of energy.

"It's important to cover yourself financially so you don't depend on acting for your money. Acting is my job, but not my income. That leaves me free to make better choices about the acting I do. Of course, it's every poor actor's dream to be in a nationally televised commercial, but the competition is brutal.

"I've been an extra in lots of commercials. I'm a body that walks by, but you don't see my face or hear my voice. If you're an extra, you just get day rate. If you're on-camera, you can get well paid, and you can get residuals if they use the commercial for long enough. And if you're serious about being an actor, do whatever you have to to get into a union like the Screen Actors Guild."

How did you get the job?

"I came to New York after college, took every workshop I could, and went to every audition I could get into. I spent a fortune having new head shots made every time I changed my persona. I started as a leading man, but now I mostly go out for the 'goofy guy' parts."

Naming the Postmoderns

Perhaps if we could come up with a catchy name for the generation of people who have come to working age during a time when it's so hard to find work, more people in older generations would abandon their preconceived notions and appreciate the dilemmas these young people face.

What to call the generation that hits the job market near the end of the twentieth century? Perhaps "DJs" because they are faced with a de-jobbed economy. "PoCa," short for Post Career, is catchy. "The Downsized" has a certain grim appropriateness. How about "PoMo," short for Postmodern—or Poor More.

65   🦉   Lighting Designer

Jay is a lighting designer. He has designed the lighting for several restaurants and clubs.

"Once you start thinking about lighting, you notice it everywhere—mostly poorly done. And there's no need for that. Lighting is one of the best ways to define a space, and there's all sorts of technology available. I hate to say it, but the Europeans are way ahead of us in this regard.

"The more I work at this, the more I see light. Light, and how it's used, is what makes great paintings and buildings. And some of the finest uses of light are in old black-and-white movies. I think that providing the proper mix of lighting would make a lot of people healthier. Certainly you can diminish seasonal affective disorder. We have the technology to do so much better with light; it's time for us to start realizing what we can do.

"I'd like to start working more with architects. Right now I'm working with a lot of interior designers, and most of the work is retrofit. I'd like to see good, dramatic lighting designed in from the start, as part of a building's concept. I think people are ready for that."

How did you get the job?

"I learned about lighting as a theater techie. I have a burn scar on my wrist from the first spotlight I ever pointed—ninth grade. I was up in the balcony, hand pointing this thing that was about as big as I was, and changing gels to change the mood in the production of *Our Town*. I got my first restaurant job because they wanted something theatrical, and that's what I did. I got written up, and handed out hundreds of reprints of the story."

Moving for Work

It's worth thinking about how willing you are to move. The best way to maximize your job possibilities is to move to where the work is.

Gayle knew she wanted no part of the business world. She wanted to work in a public policy area, either for a nonprofit or for part of the government. She also wanted to stay in her home state of Oregon. The problem was that Oregon's capital is sleepy, conservative Salem, and there aren't a lot of nonprofits headquartered in the state. While she was looking for a job in Oregon, she volunteered for politicians and political campaigns.

It was clear that New York and Washington offered her a much better chance of finding the right kind of job. She found that job in steps: first taking a short-term job in New York, then moving up to a full-time job, then moving to exactly the kind of place she wanted.

On the other hand, Sylvester graduated from a high-powered MBA program—one of the best. Now, more than a year later, he's a waiter. The problem? He's unwilling to live anywhere other than Denver, Colorado.

It may be easier for you to move at this stage of your life than it will be later. Moving gets more expensive later. You'll have more stuff—and your friends will probably no longer be willing to help you move.

Don't rely on statistics alone to help you make a moving decision. Washington, D.C., is projected to see job growth in the next decade, but we wouldn't assume that it's going to be a fair and open market. Joplin, Missouri, has one of the lowest costs of living in the country, but it's not for everyone. The New York area has high prices, expensive homes, long commutes—and lots of New Yorkers wouldn't think of living anywhere else.

66 🦉 Gardener

Billy was on his way to becoming an executive, but he's taken a detour. Now he's a gardener.

"The whole college thing backfired, from my parents' point of view. I was all on track to be Mr. Success, but by the time I got out, I had developed some of my own ideas about the respectability of sweat and the importance of being close to nature.

"I think it was Thoreau that put me over the top. I figured he was right about nature and he was right about civil disobedience. Only, in this case it's more familial disobedience. But it really was all of it. Botany, geology, reading the transcendentalists—they all pointed this way.

"I have five clients, and I spend the equivalent of a week at each house. I get job offers all the time, but I'm committed to the gardens that I'm tending. What they want from me are extravagant displays of flowers, and they get that. What they also get is organic gardening, and some portion of each garden devoted to something edible."

How did you get the job?

"I rode around town on my bicycle until I spotted an old house being painted. I rang the doorbell and told the lady that if she really wanted her house to look good, she should plant some flowers. It was an incredibly obnoxious thing to do, but the house was architecturally weird, so I figured the owner might be unusual. She is unusual. She has never called me by name; she just calls me Mr. Organic."

"Everything Has Changed Except Our Thinking."
—Albert Einstein

As usual, Einstein is right. So copy this statement and post it somewhere where you'll see it often.

- When you start dreaming of a lifetime career, read it.
- When you start thinking that a corporation will take care of you, read it.
- When you are tempted to beat up on yourself for not having a job, read it.
- When you're tempted to restrict your job hunting to just answering newspaper ads, read it.
- When people ask you why you haven't yet found a job, make them read it.

McJobs

What if you just want to buy some time while you decide whether to go to graduate school, or to move back home and take over the farm, or to bother to try for a ''career''-type job?

Or, what if you want a break after all that college?

Something fast and easy sounds good—you want a McJob.

67 🦉 Switchboard

Vicki works facing a big switchboard in a little cramped room.

"This is the ultimate dead-end job. Switchboards are being eliminated all over town. But the partners here like having a real voice answer the phone, and an intelligent person at the switchboard to make the clients feel cared for.

"And I do a good job of making sure that people aren't left hanging. I know which calls are customers, and which are salespeople. I recognize voices. I know who's sleeping with who, and I'm not telling.

"I'm going to be very sad when this job gets eliminated. It's so much better than being stuck at home. In a way, I'm the heart of the company; I'm its voice. People who call in ask where I am when someone relieves me at lunchtime."

How did you get the job?

"They had had a lot of trouble finding a switchboard operator who would stay put and do the job. They always got claustrophobic and wandered around. I'm in a wheelchair, so I convinced them that I wouldn't be likely to wander, and I told them that my father would do the carpentry to widen the door to the switchboard room if they bought the materials. (They paid him anyway; he'd like more work like that.)

"The hard part was getting the job agency to send me over. They were afraid the company would get mad at them, but they did the right thing."

The ADA—Americans With Disabilities Act

The ADA—Americans With Disabilities Act—is starting to have an impact on jobs and the job market. As with many new laws, the exact implications of the act are being worked out on a case-by-case basis in court, but the gist of the law, as regards employment, is that an employer should not discriminate against you because of a disability if there is a reasonable accommodation that would make it possible for you to do a job that you are in other ways capable of doing.

Many employers are aware of this law, and are becoming increasingly willing to make accommodations for employees. Don't assume you can't get a job until you've suggested the accommodation you'd need and been turned down. If you want to talk to someone about what accommodations other people have requested and received, or if you feel you've been unfairly turned down, you may want to talk to a lawyer.

68 🦉 Nude Modeling

Carryl gets paid for sitting still for long periods of time. The catch is that she does it nude.

"I started nude modeling in college. I get a lot of work because I'm a good model. I'm no raving beauty, but I spent my childhood studying modern dance and ballet, so I have the discipline and muscles needed to hold a pose, and I know how to choose poses that I can hold.

"It's almost like a form of meditation, although not quite that relaxed. But my mind definitely wanders and works on other problems. I'm not really there in the room while I'm posing.

"I only pose in the studios at the university, and only for people who are interested in art. You'd have to be crazy to do nude modeling out in the real world with all the sleazes. It's never caused me any problems, although one guy nearly died of embarrassment when we were introduced at a party. I had never noticed him before. He turned bright red."

How did you get the job?

"It was posted on the art department bulletin board at college."

And You Think You've Had a Lot of Jobs

For a good perspective on working, read Claudia Shear's *Blown Sideways Through Life*. Writing the book was her sixty-sixth job. She knows a lot about how depressing and oppressive jobs can be, but she manages to keep her sense of humor and dignity, despite it all.

She's probably up to job seventy-five by now. She also made her show/book into a TV special, and was a guest star on the situation comedy "Friends."

Part of Claudia's message is that everyone is important, that everyone has a story, and that you can learn something from everyone. She's someone worth listening to. After all, she may have left a lot of jobs—but she's also gotten a lot of them.

69 🦉 Cabbie

Roger drives a cab. He claims to be the last English-speaking cabdriver in New York.

"Driving can be good money, and it's always good stories. I'm writing up the stories I hear and experience and I'm going to make them into a movie someday. Getting the license was pretty easy—I already knew the streets.

"You learn a lot about yourself while driving. I thought I was a nice, liberal guy when I started driving. I'm not. I don't pick up old people because they take forever getting in and out of the cab, and they're lousy tippers, but I pick up hookers because they tip well. You leave something valuable in this cab and it's mine. And I don't pick up groups of young black kids. Once I drove three girls to Harlem and they jumped out without paying. The second time two black guys robbed me at gunpoint. So, it may be illegal, but I'm not getting shot.

"One thing you gotta say for this job: it's always something different. I've had opera singers rehearse in the cab. Lots of ladies change clothes in the cab, and the occasional couple will use the back of the cab as a motel room for a quickie. And last year a producer left a music festival and handed me a bag of demo CDs. All that's amusing. But I've also driven a lot of crying people to hospitals, police stations, and funeral homes.

"I really am going to write a movie about this job. Half the people talk like I'm not here anyway, so I'm like a camera. I had two financial guys discussing a merger in the backseat the other day. If I had money to invest, I could have bought the company being acquired. It's amazing."

How did you get the job?

"I got my hack license and called the number on the back of a cab."

The Declining Middle

If you have a degree, but you're working harder and not getting rich, you're not alone. Demographically the college educated are part of what's called the declining middle—the middle class that's losing ground. This is highly unusual. As you'll remember from your Survey of Modern History course, the middle class is generally always rising (although it never seems to get to where it's going.) Not now. The generations that are hitting the job market now are facing a new set of rules—where the young are more likely to be poor than the aged, and where many people are likely to end up living less well than their parents. To put it into economic terms, a lot of us are experiencing downward mobility.

For some perspective on how and why this has happened, you can read *The Overworked American: The Unexpected Decline of Leisure,* by Juliet B. Schor, a Harvard economist (1991, BasicBooks).

70 🦉 Bike Messenger

Glen wanted a job where he could stay in shape while he trained as a marathoner. He became a bike messenger.

"The Boston area's weird. A lot of times a bike can beat a car, and there's no parking problem. So bike messengers make sense. Except for the fact that we have to contend with the craziest drivers on earth.

"My pet peeves are people who call us before they're ready and have us wait around while they get the package together, and receptionists who won't let me use the phone or the bathroom. There's this odd assumption that just because I'm a bike messenger, I must be a criminal or a moron. It doesn't occur to them that I'm as well educated as they are, and could be working in an office if I wanted to.

"I'm not going to keep at this much longer. I am in shape, true. But I'm also getting banged up a lot. No matter how carefully you look and listen, some fool's going to open a car door in front of you and you'll break some bones. Meanwhile, I'm stashing the money."

How did you get the job?

"I looked in the phone book under messengers."

Why People Won't Tell You How to Get a Job

People won't tell you the secret because they don't know they know it. They all think that the fact that they got a job through the former college roommate of the best friend of their uncle's partner's mistress is the exception and not worth talking about. But connection chains like that are the rule, not the exception.

While people won't tell you how to get a job, there are a lot of books that will point out job options you never thought of. One good resource is

The Whole Work Catalog
The New Careers Center
1515 23rd Street
Box 339-CT
Boulder, Colorado 80306
1-800-634-9024

This catalog is full of books with titles like *Careers for Sports Nuts, Careers for History Buffs,* and *Law Enforcement Careers.*

71 🦉 Guard

Mike wears a blue uniform and walks around a construction site at night with a big flashlight.

"This job is the biggest joke imaginable. All it takes to be a guard is to not have a felony on your record. I walk around at set intervals, and I'm supposed to call the police if there are any problems. That's it. The rest of the time I read or write. I have gotten an amazing amount of reading done.

"I have no real interest in protecting their property, and certainly wouldn't get hurt doing it. But, realistically, they don't expect me to do anything like that. I think having a guard posted is an insurance requirement.

"Even though I wouldn't fight, no one knows that, so my presence is a deterrent. Especially since I've taken to bringing my dog, Veng, to work for company. I might not fight, but I pity anyone who attacked me while Veng was watching."

How did you get the job?

"I called the number from an ad in the paper."

Scam Alert

When people really want something, they become a target for scam operators. And, since job hunters really want jobs, there are, inevitably, some nasty folks who prey on them. Before handing cash over to someone who promises to help you find a job, check them out. If you go to a job seminar and you start feeling pressured, remind yourself not to sign or pay for anything on the spot. If it's a real opportunity, it'll probably still be there in twenty-four hours.

72 🦉 Housepainter

Dick is a housepainter.

"What's there to say? I paint houses, inside and out. I don't do art, but I do trim. I can paint with a brush or a roller, whichever you please, and I can use stain or latex, and I'll even use oil if you want.

"The oddest job we've done lately was a historic house where we weren't allowed to use power tools. The oddest one ever was the one where the ladies at the pool next door liked to skinny-dip. That's the only job I've ever been on where the oldest painters claimed the right to do the eaves. I hate eaves—that's where the wasps' nests are.

"This is honest work. No pretensions to it. I didn't need to go to college to do it, but that's not why I went to college. I work hard, drink hard, and sleep well. I work for other contractors because I have no interest in running a business. I call my lifestyle 'short form' because that's how I pay my taxes."

How did you get the job?

"I started painting houses in college. By the time summer started, it was the only summer job left. Once you're a painter, it's easy to get work. The same guys keep calling me."

The Top Ten Anti-Work Anthems

Yes, this book is meant to tell you how to find your spot. But there's nothing wrong with an occasional dose of rebellion—especially if you are in job mode, not career mode. When you're bored or bothered by work, trying singing one of these:

1. "Bang the Drum All Day"—Todd Rundgren
2. "We Gotta Get Out of This Place"—The Animals
3. "Take This Job and Shove It"—Johnny Paycheck
4. "Workin' for a Living"—Huey Lewis and the News
5. "Smoke Two Joints"—The Toys
6. "9 to 5"—Dolly Parton
7. "Back on the Chain Gang"—Pretenders
8. "Sixteen Tons"—Tennessee Ernie Ford
9. "Working for the Weekend"—Loverboy
10. "Proud Mary"—Creedence Clearwater Revival

73 🦉 Bank Teller

Celestine is a bank teller for a federal credit union in Washington, D.C.

"I know banks are doing everything they can to steer people away from banks, but they'll always need a few tellers. My customers like the experience of handing their money over to a real person. I say 'my' customers because I've seen a lot of them let people go ahead of them just so they can come to my window. I always smile, and I know a lot of them by name. I was out sick once and several of them asked me how I was when I came back.

"I also have to admit that I get pleasure from handling all that money. I know it's not mine, but it's still fun to hold it and count it.

"I'm careful. My drawer always comes out right."

How did you get the job?

"A friend works at the bank, and she told me about the opening."

Forget "References Available Upon Request"

Lots of resumés end with the line "References Available Upon Request." There's no problem with having that line there, but that's not the way to *think* about your references. You don't wait for references to be requested, you use them in advance, to get you into doors.

In sales, referrals are the best because when you are referred by someone, the folks you are referred to are presold; they already have a reason to believe in you. Same thing in job hunting.

74 🦉 Dispatcher

Shirelle is the voice that crackles over the radio in the cabs of a fleet of trucks in the midwest. Some of the truckers are literally three times heavier than she is, but they act as if they are terrified of her.

"It's a pretty simple job, and I run it fairly, for the most part. But it wouldn't be a good idea to cross me or to argue with me. I have a long memory. That doesn't mean the guys can't swear at me; it just means they can't disobey.

"I have management's total confidence. Stuff gets where it's meant to go, the fleet is well used, and people don't tend to goof off. We have a great safety record, and great documentation. They live in fear of my annual vacation. Something always screws up."

How did you get the job?

"I was working in the plant and there was a little sex discrimination problem and they had to find another place for me. I think they thought I would melt down if I had to order around a bunch of burly truckers. Haven't yet met one as scary as my father."

Most Jobs Aren't Fun

If a job were that much fun, people would do it for themselves, or other people would do it for free. If you're going to get paid, you're going to be asked to do something that most people regard as not fun or can't do, or something that involves some loss of your freedom.

On the other hand, it does happen on occasion that people get jobs that are fun for them. They're happy, and so is

How to Make Use of a Useless Degree

everyone else, because happy people are often easier to work with than miserable people, and happy people are often more productive.

And sometimes while the work isn't fun, the group you work with can be. Think of the book/movie/TV show *M*A*S*H*. Those people were doing grisly work in horrible circumstances. But a lot of the time they managed to have fun. The reverse happens, too. You can be doing work that should be fun, but working with people who spoil it for you.

Many jobs get to be more fun as you get to know the people better and as you get better at what you do. It feels nice to know you can do something well, and you waste less emotional energy worrying about mistakes. Of course, some jobs stay miserable for as long as you stay at them.

75 🦉 Bookstore Clerk

Chad works in a little bookstore in San Francisco.

"I would never work at a chain bookstore, but I'm happy, for the moment, at this one. I like the fact that it sells both new and used books. That makes it smell the way a bookstore should smell. I tried a job as a secretary at an engineering firm, but I missed intellectual discussion. I could feel my brain rotting, day by day. Engineers are generally very narrow-focus.

"I am the only one of my friends who can honestly say that I use the stuff I studied in college. They all make more than I do, but they all seem to envy me. I don't envy them. I still wear what I wore in college, keep the same hours, and concern myself with the same issues."

How did you get the job?

"I asked the store owner a dozen times for work, and so did a hundred other kids. But one day when I was shopping there,

I helped a customer he was about to turn away. The customer was looking for a humor book, *The Education of Hyman Kaplan*. The customer had the author wrong, because it was published under a pseudonym, so the owner didn't find it on his list. I knew they had the book, and that it was hidden in the back row of a bottom shelf. They're so crowded, they have two rows of books on every shelf, one behind the other.

"The owner realized that I was bright, and knew his stock and his system. He also saw that it was a lot easier for me to squeeze between the piles of books and get to the bottom shelves. I got the job."

Moving for the Quality of Life

Laura is working in San Francisco. It's actually her second time working here. First she worked in New York, where she hated the pace. Then she moved to San Francisco, but she missed her East Coast family and friends. So she moved back. But then she missed the quality of life in San Francisco and crossed the country again. "It's better here," she says about San Francisco. "People are more socially conscious; there are mountains right across the bay that people want to climb. It keeps things in perspective."

A lot of people move to improve the quality of their lives. For Laura, San Francisco's the best. For Parky, however, Arizona's the only place. He likes the open spaces, the lack of cold, and the fact that he can carry a gun. If you think you might be happier in another part of the country, or the world, the years right after college are a great time to find out.

76   🦉   Property Caretaker

What's better than low rent? No rent. Brook is the caretaker of a set of cabins on a mountaintop in a park in California.

"Don't mention the exact place; we already get more traffic than is good for the environment up here.

"The job is not quite as relaxing as I thought it would be. I had talked to a friend who was a caretaker at a big estate, and he was getting a lot of painting done, taking all his bottled up urges to communicate and pouring them onto canvas. But this is different. I'm constantly on call as camp counselor and nursemaid to an endless string of people, some of whom are real boneheads.

"The views are great, I love the mountain, but I think I would have more real freedom as an advertising art director, and I've been putting a portfolio together. I've shown my work to a half a dozen ad people who have shown up, and they say I have talent."

How did you get the job?

"I read about it in the *Caretaker's Gazette.*"

The Blurred Borderline

In case your Uncle Fritz asks why all the kids are so lazy today and practically no one goes through school in four years straight the way he did (with the G.I. Bill picking up a lot of his costs), part of the answer is that jobs no longer start after college; they are very likely to start *in* college. Working is one of the only ways to meet the cost of college.

And even if the jobs you have during college don't lead to full-time paid employment after college, they are a part of the important process of learning what kind of work you like and what kind you don't like.

Studies done on veterans who return to college after some time out generally showed that they got more out of college than their younger classmates, so taking more than four years might actually lead to a better education.

Many older people went through college in four straight years because they knew that if they took some time off, they could lose their "student deferment" and get drafted. That's one of the few pressures that people of your generation didn't face, so you had even less reason to go through in four straight years.

77 🦉 Convenience Store Clerk

Marty works at a convenience store.

"I got tired of my parents always ragging on me to get a job, so I went out and took the first one I found. I work nights, they work days, and the house hasn't run out of milk for the breakfast cereal since I started. We get along much better now.

"I think they thought that I felt that I was better then they were because I had gone to college. This cleared things up. A convenience store clerk does not think they're better than anyone else."

How did you get the job?

"My father came home all sarcastic one night and asked why I didn't just go work at the Cumberland Farms store where he had seen a Help Wanted sign. It seemed easier to take the job than to argue or start job hunting."

Perspective

If you're thinking of taking a job as a clerk, rent the movie *Clerks* first.

Although it's not an issue in the movie, one of the issues that people working as clerks in all-night stores must confront is what they'll do if someone comes in to rob the store. Which raises the broader question of how much risk you should be willing to take on for your boss. Some employers take advantage of the fact that many young people are relatively fearless and ask these young workers to take on hazardous duties. Make up your own mind as to what you are ready to do, but, remember, as a rule, the riskier the job, the more you should get paid to do it.

78　Receptionist

Lindy is a receptionist at a large industrial manufacturing concern.

"I don't type, don't make copies, don't do meetings. I sit here from 9 to 10:30, from 10:45 to 12, from 1 to 3, and from 3:15 to 5, and not a minute more. I'm so pleasant to the boss it's nauseating, but I'm brutal with the messengers, who always come here and always have to go down the elevator, and up the other bank of elevators to get to the mail room.

"I do keep the magazines neat, but that's because I want to. And they think I'm wonderful because I take money from petty cash every week to buy fresh flowers.

"I had two big fantasies. One was to come into work with my nose ring in, which I will do on my last day here. The other one has already come true. It involved me and my girlfriend and this overdesigned desk. Which is why I'm able to smile and be so sweet here all the time."

"I bribed the office manager—a friend of mine leases them their copiers, so I knew the manager was on the take."

What Use Is Your Parachute?

What Color Is Your Parachute is a great book for career changers. But just as you can't use a parachute when you're still in the basement, the book isn't all that helpful if you, like Lindy, don't really give a damn what you do to make money.

If you're just working a job to get money, ignore all the literature (parts of this book included) that's aimed at people who want advancement, fulfillment, and stability, as well as money.

By not caring about a "career," you'll be breaking a lot of middle-class taboos, and you're likely to hear a lot about how you're "squandering your potential." But you're also a lot less likely to be upset when you lose one job and have to take another one, as long as you find the new one quickly.

FOOT IN THE DOOR

Lindy is a receptionist, and it's a "McJob." But Sally is also a receptionist and it's a "foot in the door." What's going on?

The answer is that there are a lot of jobs like temping, being a secretary, or working in the mail room that you could approach as a way of passing time and getting cash, or as a way of getting into a company and finding out what you have to do to get promoted.

The following five people are looking to move up.

79 🦉 Receptionist

Sally is a receptionist at a small, but growing, sales promotion and licensing firm.

"I have this job for five months while the receptionist is out on maternity leave. And I figure that's just long enough to make myself indispensable. I'm a natural for licensing—I have a great sense of apparel, of marketing, and of retailing. I just need a chance and some experience.

"I've let them know that I want to work, and they're giving me a lot of typing and collating to do. I've learned their project management software and the presentation software they use.

"The top client knows that I'll get him answers faster than his account exec, who's a little flaky, and can't seem to do anything without writing a memo about it. And they're talking about getting a temp in next week so I can work in the back for a big presentation. I'd say my plan is working."

How did you get the job?

"I cold called at all of the businesses in this area. My priority is to work near where my boyfriend works so we can continue to get along with just one car."

Ways to Make Yourself Indispensable

- Change the toner.
- Know the security codes for building access.
- Do expense reports.
- Fax stuff.
- Get to know the client.

- Learn the billing codes.
- Learn how to get cash advances.
- Get car vouchers.
- Learn the filing system.
- Get to know the suppliers.
- Hand deliver stuff.
- Make travel arrangements.
- Have aspirin.
- Have Band-Aids.
- Know the Fed Ex cutoff time.

80 🦉 Temp

Max isn't a temp, but he was, and he recommends it as a way of breaking into a company.

"A temp job was the fastest and easiest way for me to get a full-time job. I knew I was good, and I just needed a chance to show it. I performed well at my first temp job and was made a 'regular' employee in the Accounting Department after three months. Three raises and two promotions later I'm still here.

"I started at a much higher level than I would have if I had come in any other way. I knew the company and I had proof that I could do the job. Besides, the temp company had paid me only a third of what they were collecting, so they had set a pretty high value on my services."

How did you get the job?

"I just told you."

About Temping

As more and more companies "downsize," and get "leaner and meaner" by firing employees for whom they have to pay benefits, the market for temporary workers grows and grows. Temps aren't just secretaries and receptionists: there are temp computer programmers, temp drivers, even temp executives.

It can be argued that temps are being exploited: deprived of benefits they deserve and given cruddy jobs. One of the places where this case is made most strongly is in a 'zine, a small privately published publication, called *Temp Slave.* It's available from someone called "Keffo" at P.O. Box 8284, Madison, WI 53708-8284, for $2 an issue or $7.00 for a four-issue subscription. If you're going to temp, it's worth a read. Keffo's comment about mentioning his publication in this book was "They need to know it's ugly out there in work-land."

If you want to do temp work, consider registering with more than one temp agency. The big agencies, such as Kelly and Manpower, often have exclusive relationships with large companies, so if you are only talking to one temp agency, you might miss some opportunities.

For the record, according to the January/February 1995 issue of *Solidarity,* the magazine that the United Auto Workers sends to its members, only 8 percent of temp agency workers have health coverage, only 3 percent of them get sick pay, and 77 percent of them earn less than $9 an hour.

If you are temping, be very aware of your tax status. If the temp agency is withholding taxes from what they pay you, you should be fine when tax time rolls around. But if they aren't withholding from you, you have to put aside money and pay estimated taxes.

81 🦉 Intern

Margaret is doing her second internship. She thinks it's a smart move.

"You need to do internships, because college has nothing to do with work. You don't know whether you'll like a certain kind of work or a certain company, and getting inside the company for a while is a great way to find out.

"My first internship saved me from making a big mistake. I thought that working in the Marketing Communications Department of an insurance company would be an exciting, but very secure, place. The way things are going I thought they'd be positioning themselves as a more active financial and service institution. I was way off. The company I was at is nowhere near that point yet, and they are far from secure.

"This internship is working better. I'm at a bank card company, and they're busy figuring out how to accept and protect payments on the Internet."

How did you get the job?

"In each case, I've gone in from the top. I call it my golf club strategy. I meet these guys at my parents' golf club and chat with them. The higher the rank of the executive who recommends you, the greater the odds that you'll be given interesting work."

About Internships

One way to find out if you and a profession or company are right for each other is to be an intern for a while. Interns don't get paid much, but there's generally an unspoken agreement that you're supposed to be given meaningful, relevant work instead of all the grunt work. (Don't count on it.) Unlike school, on an internship, no one is paid to teach you. You either help or you're in the way.

The postgraduate internship is becoming more common—for a lot of people it's the only way to get entry and experience. That's painful—but a reflection of the market.

What it amounts to is volunteering. You may have done an internship during school—but then you were getting credit, which may be more valuable than the stipend you are offered, if you are offered one.

Although it's aimed at students, *The Princeton Review's Student Access Guide to America's Top 100 Internships,* by Mark Oldman and Samer Hamadeh, (Villard Books) is still a good resource book about interning opportunities.

82 Secretary

Mollie has taken a job as a secretary. She had set her sights higher, but this was what she could get.

"I made it clear when I took this job that I was taking it as a first step into sales management. They made it clear that they expected at least a one-year commitment to remaining a secretary from me. Fair enough.

"What makes me think it's possible is the fact that one of the top people here started as the president's secretary. She's positioned to be president herself someday. It shows that there's no prejudice against secretaries and no prejudice against women.

"Being a secretary is a good place to learn. The only things I don't get to read are the blue 'Confidential' envelopes. By the end of a year here, I should know what makes the place tick, and they should know that I'm underused as a secretary."

"I got an interview through my 'mentor'—a businesswoman who's one of this company's clients. I told them I wanted to start as a junior executive. They told me I could be a secretary. I said, 'No thanks,' and walked out. Two weeks later, I called to apologize and ask if the secretary position was still open."

Comments from a Hiring Executive

Mr. Lonsdale is in the process of interviewing to hire two people: a secretary and an account executive.

"Don't expect an hour-long interview from me. I know some people in this company do that, but I can't imagine what they say. I'm going to know whether or not I want to hire you in the first ten minutes. I might stretch the interview to twenty or thirty minutes, but an hour—never.

"For the secretary position—which we now call administrative assistant, but who are we kidding?—I want to know that you can stay cool, that you can speak well, that you can read bad handwriting (mine's the worst), and that you understand that this is not a strict nine-to-five deal and that, while I try to promote all my people, I'm looking for a secretary who will stay in that job for a year or more.

"I'll be measuring you against Charlene, the best secretary I ever had. She had come from a law firm where she had supported three partners, so this was a breeze for her. She came to the interview in a bright red coat, so I knew she had personality, and when I asked her about reading bad writing, she read me the memo on my desk, which was upside down to her.

"For the account position, I'm looking for a little more. Mainly, I'm looking for someone who will solve problems, rather than create them. I've got too many clients and too many responsibilities, and I want someone who can take some of that off my hands.

"If I have to hand-hold you every step of the way, or if you're not a self-starter, you are no good to me. I'm traveling a lot, and I have to know that you'll keep working and take care of business while I'm gone.

"I'll be measuring that person against the early performance of the two senior account people I have now. The first one, Tad, came in here for his interview, pointed at the stack of billing I had on my credenza, and said, 'Why are you doing that if you're a vice president? I could do that for you.' He was right. We could have stopped there, one minute into the interview; he was hired.

"The second is Tracy. Her interview was a bit longer. Her experience wasn't a perfect fit, so I had to probe a little longer. Her recent jobs seemed pretty boring, so I wasn't sure she'd be able to cope with the madness of this place. But, before that, she had worked as the manager of her family's restaurant, so I asked her what was the hardest thing she ever had to do there. She told me that a waiter had died in the men's room during the lunch hour rush and she had to figure out how to get him out of there without alarming the customers. I knew right away that she could cope with this place."

83 🦉 Mail Room Worker

Graham is the only guy in his mail room who wears a tie every day.

"Starting in the mail room is a time-honored tradition. All sorts of people started in the mail room at William Morris, for example. This isn't William Morris, but it's still entertainment, so I have to show that I have style.

"I'm not sure how the break will come, but it will. The other guys teased me at first, but they're behind me. I get to do the deliveries to the top two floors and I'm the one who carries things into meetings. I am, I'm pretty sure, the only one from the mail room who the boss knows by name.

"The only thing I'm afraid of is someone asking me to fulfill one of the other time-honored mail room functions: getting drugs or hookers for them."

How did you get the job?

"I made an appointment with Personnel, and I told them I would take any job to be a part of this company."

Don't Resent That Good Suit

For a number of jobs, you will want to get a good suit for interviewing. Even jobs where you would never wear a suit. But it's not as bad as a prom dress or a graduation gown—which get used once and thereafter are only good for Halloween parties. Often it takes three or four interviews to get a job. And often you have to try at several different places before you land a job. Plus, as long as it fits, you can break the suit out for weddings and funerals.

With the cost of occasional dry cleaning, the suit will never be as cheap or convenient as renting bowling shoes. But it's likely to get a fair amount of use (and no one else gets to wear it).

If you're looking for an "interview suit," don't make yourself too crazy over the details. If it's well made, fits comfortably, and is in good, clean condition, it's probably fine. And remember, natural fibers not only tend to look better; they also breathe better when you're sweating through that interview.

START A BUSINESS

A number of the people already mentioned have started their own businesses. A lot of people find it's the best way they can find a spot for themselves.

No matter how much companies talk about new structures, their structure tends to remain a pyramid—with lots of people at the bottom and fewer people at the top. But lots of people would like to be at the top. That leads to problems. Not only will scads of people not be able to grow up to be President of the United States, no matter what their parents told them, they won't even be able to grow up to be assistant vice presidents of Fortune 500 companies. But they can become something even more elevated: "Founder."

84 🦉 Caterer

Bill would like to have a restaurant someday, but for now he caters.

"I needed to stay near home because my mother is old and alone since my father died. But there was no way to find a job. So I created one. I became a caterer. I cut a deal with the church. They had a big, industrial kitchen in the parish hall that was never used. I provide them with a banquet every two weeks, and I can use the kitchen whenever I want.

"It turns out the banquets were the best advertising I could have done. The town was tired of the traditional turkey à la king or spaghetti options, and I'm giving them all the variety they want.

"The best part is that Mom is acting ten years younger. Before, she was drawing into herself and napping and playing a lot of solitaire. Now she's half-running the business, and she comes along to a lot of the events."

Best source of customers?

"The church dinner."

Relocate or Create

If you aren't willing to relocate, you may have to be willing to create your own job. Creating a business is always risky. Many businesses fail because they are undercapitalized. (And if you had all that capital, you'd be a lot less worried to begin with.)

If you do decide to start a business, see what advice you can get from the

U.S. Small Business Administration
1441 L Street, NW

Washington, DC 20416
Hotline: (800) 368-5855

Our experience with the SBA is that it's not much help. They have all sorts of programs, including guaranteed loans, but their definition of a small business seems to be one that only has a few million dollars. But they are worth trying, nonetheless. Maybe they act as a screener: the people who are determined enough to get helpful information are the ones who have the drive to succeed in a start-up venture.

One strategy that might help you get more from the SBA is to find out the location of the Small Business Development Center nearest you, and go there and see what publications and resources they can offer you.

85 🦉 Car Detailer

Vinnie's got a growing business. He details cars. He comes to your house or place of business, gets your car, and returns it, cleaner than it's been in years.

"It didn't cost me anything to get started in the business. I already had all the stuff for keeping my own cars clean. I'm kind of a nut about this. We're talking custom-made vacuum nozzles and dental picks as well as the usual Q-tips and chemicals.

"I got started by accident. My car is kind of known around here, so my girlfriend asked me if I'd put a Vinnie Car Cleaning into a charity auction at her school. I figured it would go for $20–$25 dollars. That's where it started, but some lady bought it for her husband for $250. Now I'm not saying that it's worth that to most people, but I realized I could charge $75. I started with the other bidders from the auction.

"Most of my business is gifts—it's a real big gift for the man who has everything. And one traveling salesman, who is a pig, let me tell you, has me do his car each month. His company pays."

Best source of customers?

"An article in the local paper."

　　　　　　　　　　How to Make Use of a Useless Degree

Titles

One of the ways people meet their need for elevated titles is to start their own ventures. For example, Vinnie could call himself Chairman, President, Principal, Honcho, Big Cheese, Poobah, or Big Enchilada.

Titles may seem silly, and fundamentally undemocratic to you (they are), but a lot of the people you will talk to in your job search will have worked quite hard to get the titles they have, and may be quite proud of them. Make it a point to get titles right. It's hard, because there are no standards: at some companies, being vice president means you're the number three person. At other companies, VPs are as common as weeds, and the title only gets impressive when you become a senior vice president or an executive vice president. In most places, the title "partner" is important: it means you are, in some sense, an owner. And, as impressive as "president" sounds, presidents are generally outranked by chairmen and chairwomen, and chief executive officers (CEOs).

The best way to get titles right is to ask people for their business card—there are only a few companies that don't use people's titles on their cards. (And very few companies will let people without titles have cards. Getting cards is a real mark that you've made it in some places.)

While you're struggling along waiting to get your first title, and even after you've gotten a few, it's good to remember the Italian proverb that "When the game is over, the king and the pawn go back into the same box." Under all the titles, we're all just people.

86 🦉 Cat Sitter

Alma runs a cat sitting service.

"I'm a cat person, and I know how other cat people get about their cats: crazy. So here's my service. I go to the cat's home, spend an hour talking and playing with the cat, feed it, and check the litter box. And the cat owner can call me at home at a designated time at night to get a report. $25 a visit, $30 on weekends.

"I thought it was exorbitant, but I guess not. One woman whose cat won't eat when he's lonely pays me for double shifts, and she wants me to watch TV with her cat. Some days I have eight different cats to visit, and I work, of course, seven days a week."

Best source of customers?

"Other cat owners."

Drug Testing

Drug testing is, at best, an unnecessary invasion of privacy. Companies would be much better off with skill-based tests that relate to the actual tasks at hand. If you go without sleep for forty-eight hours, even though you can pass a drug test, you shouldn't be driving a truck. But lots of companies do drug testing, so you'd better be ready for it.

If drug testing is a concern for you, try to find out through the grapevine whether a company you want to apply at requires it. There's also probably some way to ask this question via the Internet, if the company is big enough. It's not a question you want to ask of the screening interviewer in Personnel.

Derek didn't think about this and was caught by a sneaky interviewer who asked him what he wanted as salary and benefits, met his request, and then mentioned the drug testing and gave him a permission slip to sign. Just because they are in the people side of the business, not all HR people are nice and understanding. A lot of them are zealous about catching and weeding out the "wrong kinds" of people.

87 🦉 Frozen Yogurt Entrepreneur

Until recently, Darryl had a little business that leased soft serve frozen yogurt machines to cafeterias.

"It looked like an opportunity. I lease the machines to cafeterias that serve over a thousand people a day, and make money off supplying the material that goes in them. The numbers were all there. So I got some people to back me and went into business.

"What I didn't count on was that once they had our nice machines, the cafeterias were happy to violate the agreement and get supplies from someone else. So I'm stuck doing all the maintenance, but not getting the income I deserve. After a while, the machines started breaking and I had trouble getting parts. I finally bailed out. On balance, I paid myself nothing for three years of work."

Best source of customers?

"Hospitals."

The Home Office Deduction

If you work out of your home, one of the things you may want to think about is whether you can deduct part of your home from your taxes. The Internal Revenue Service has strict rules about this, so it's not something to fool around with. But if there is part of your home that is used exclusively for work, and you have enough income to make deductions a concern, and if you have enough other deductions to make filing an itemized tax return (as opposed to using the standard form) worthwhile, look into this.

88 🦉 Stylist

Chloe is a stylist. She finds and purchases or rents props.

"I got out of college with the same skills I had when I went in: a sense of style and an ability to shop. Which, as far as I could figure out, qualified me to be a doctor's wife. But one day as I'm returning something at Bloomingdale's, I notice that the woman in front of me is returning a bunch of stuff, both men's and women's, and it's clear that the store people know her, that this is a regular thing. So we start talking.

"She has about eight bags from other stores, and I tag along and help her carry. I had nothing to do, anyway. She offers me $50 to help her shop. We hit a bunch of the best stores, returning and picking up new stuff. Then we go to a couple of fashion houses where they're loaning her stuff. By now I've got the picture of what she does, and I know I could do it.

"The next day, she gives me $100 to help her load some racks of clothes and go to a shoot. We help these gorgeous models get dressed, saying, 'That belt's all wrong, try this; don't tie the scarf that way, try these shoes.' The next day, we're returning the stuff that didn't get used and figuring out the bill.

"Six months later, I'm in business for myself."

Best source of customers?

"Repeat business. Clients ask agencies to hire me. I always buy a few extra things in the client's size, not the model's. They never seem to get returned, and they come out of the shoot budget."

What to Wear

Chloe says that if you can't afford her $500-a-day-plus expenses fee so she can tell you personally what would work best for you, you should follow these general rules:

- Dress like a news anchor.
- Dress the way you want to be treated (no—not diapers).
- Dress two levels above the job you are interviewing for.

89 🦉 Personal Trainer

Jackie is a personal trainer.

"It's pretty simple. You sell what you know, and working out is what I know. I'm not just some fluff head who likes to bounce around, I've done a lot of studying. I know a lot about muscles, bones, and all that.

"Besides, my clients aren't ready to go to an aerobics class. They are generally people who hated gym class and locker rooms, and who are incredibly ashamed of their bodies. Getting slowly into shape in the privacy of their own home is their only shot.

"I'm very discreet. I don't advertise. I get business by referrals, and from spas. I've visited a lot of spas and met with their fitness directors. They know that I can help their visitors keep the spa benefits after they leave. I come in dressed like a businesswoman, and I don't carry in any obvious equipment. And I act like a businesswoman: I charge clients full price for sessions not canceled forty-eight hours in advance.

"The biggest problem was what to charge. I started much too low. One of my clients told me that I should charge her what her shrink does, because at least I was getting results."

Best source of customers?

"My customer Briggs. Every time she goes down a dress size, I get calls from four new ladies."

Disability Insurance

When you're in business for yourself and you get sick or hurt, you lose your income. Disability insurance is designed to pay you in this circumstance. Most of the young entrepreneurs we spoke to didn't have it. It was too hard to get or too expensive.

But it is something you should at least look into if you are running your own business, and you have established a tax return track record of income. If you don't report your income for tax purposes, no one's going to insure it.

90   Book Search Service

Alex runs a book search business out of his apartment.

"It's basically a matter of combing through long lists of books offered by various sellers, and spotting ones my customers want. A lot of my competitors search by key words. I find a lot of stuff they miss, because I try and think of larger areas of interest. One customer buys books written by people who have the same last name as he does. He probably has four people searching for him. But, evidently, I'm the only one who's thought to offer him a book written *about* a member of his family.

"I don't buy the books until my customers say they want them, so I have no inventory costs. I learned that the hard way. And I pay my suppliers quickly, so they treat me well. I use the fax when I can, so I get to my customers before competitors. I usually underprice them, too. I work out of my apartment, so I don't need to mark things up as much."

Best source of customers?

"The bulk of my business comes through small ads in magazines."

Comments from Another Boss

Lance works for the Communications Department of a nationally known nonprofit organization. He's just gotten funding to add another person.

"What I'm looking for is a team player who can deal with stress. Our work isn't at one constant level: there are pushes. And when there's a mailing to get out, or something like that, I need everyone on the team to pitch in. I don't want to hear 'It's not my job' and I don't want to hear 'I'm too stressed out to help.' That drives me crazy.

"It goes without saying that I also need anyone I hire to be articulate and to have a basic command of, and commitment to, the causes we serve. They have to be able to take a call from the press, and direct it to the right person. They also have to be able to write. And they should be comfortable with technology. We use E-mail a lot, and need to start using it more.

"OK, so I'm looking for a lot. But there are a lot of good people out there, and this is a great cause."

91 🦉 House Cleaner

Bella's found a way to make a living while remaining on a resort island.

"I run a house cleaning service. I started by myself, but now, in season, I hire half a dozen helpers. To someone who grew up here, the idea of having someone else clean your house seems pretty extravagant. But what people pay to rent or buy out here is pretty extravagant.

"A lot of the rentals go by the week, and I clean before every new tenant. One house is in a divorce battle, and I clean before the place is handed from spouse to spouse. And my services are built into a lot of the all-season rentals.

"In the winter, business is a lot slower. But the owners do want to have someone out here who they can call to see how the house survived the latest storm. They also pay me to be here when repair and service people come.

"A lot of people call me just to open their houses. They get here late at night at the start of a vacation, and the place has already been aired out, there's juice and soda in the refrigerator, and flowers on the counter."

Best source of customers?

"Local realtors."

Women Who Own Businesses

Starting a business is a particularly attractive option for women, who may have a harder time rising to the top in existing organizations. Many women who have been successful with their own businesses have decided to help other women take the same route. If you are a woman thinking of starting a business, one place you might want to look for advice and mentoring is a local chapter of the National Association for Female Executives (NAFE — pronounced Naffy), 30 Irving Place, 5th Floor, N.Y., N.Y. 10003. Not all NAFE members own companies, but they are all likely to be inclined to help a young woman get one started.

For the record, *Fortune* magazine estimates that 70% of the new businesses started in the U.S.A. each year are started by women. In other words, women are founding companies at about twice the rate that men are.

Do Good

There are a lot of good reasons for doing good. While increases in productivity may be eliminating the necessity for a lot of jobs, there is no shortage, and no predicted shortage, of the number of people and organizations that could use your help.

Here are four examples of people whose daily work makes a difference.

92 🦉 Fund-Raiser

Bob gets paid to raise funds for a museum.

"I was wondering what to do with my life when I heard the local public radio station asking for volunteers to take pledges at a telethon. I had nothing better to do, so I signed up. I found that while I hate the idea of selling commercial products, I'm comfortable asking for money for organizations I believe in. That was my start. The next week I helped out at a benefit.

"I am the perfect person to be in Development, which is what we call fund-raising. I was brought up with good manners, I look respectable, and I speak rationally, but feel emotionally about my causes. I am with a museum now, and I'm close to getting a donor to underwrite a children's program."

How did you get the job?

"I showed them my dedication by devoting every spare minute I could to helping them. I told them I wanted to work for them, and I convinced them that I would raise more than enough money to cover my salary in my first month. It was a foolish statement, because that's not how organizations budget, but it impressed them, and they gave me a job the next time they had an opening."

Talk to Everyone

When you're checking out a company, information that comes from just one person isn't a good enough basis for a job decision. There's always one person who's got an unusually sweet deal, and one who prefers to gripe.

> Talk to people in different departments and they'll describe very different companies. Your best protection is to talk to as many people as possible, in as many areas as possible, as close to your own age as possible.

93   Volunteer

Nan is a big advocate of volunteering, and a typical example of the kind of path a lot of people take these days.

"When I got out of college, I had an idea that I wanted to be in publishing, so I networked through a friend and got a job as an assistant editor at a company publishing science books. It wasn't exactly what I had in mind—but it was publishing. Over the next fifteen months, I discovered that publishing was not for me, and decided that social work was what I'd like to do.

"So I went back to school to get a better academic background so I could get into one of the top social work schools in a Ph.D. program. Along the way, I learned that I enjoyed research, which I thought I would hate.

"I've volunteered as much as I could in various social work areas and, by working with them, gotten a much clearer idea of what social workers with master's degrees (MSWs) can do. I decided I didn't need a Ph.D. after all."

How did you get the job?

"I asked everyone in my department at school about their projects. When I found one that interested me, I offered my services."

Do Local Volunteer Work

Need an excuse to stay in town for a while? Think globally, and act locally. If you can afford to go without income for a while, volunteer work can be a great way to stay. And if you're motivated to volunteer, even if you take a paying job, there's no reason why you can't spend some of your time doing good works.

While doing volunteer work, people often get a clearer idea of the kind of work they like to do, and of how important money is to them. If you're really good, you can sometimes get a job with the organization you're working for. And if the organization is bad, it's easy to walk away; they're not paying you, after all. (Although they might try and guilt-trip you into staying.)

Here are some suggestions for places to volunteer:

- Hospitals always need help. Even if you can't stand the sight of blood, there are jobs like reorganizing the file room.
- Libraries often need help. So do churches and the Y.
- Public television and radio stations often need volunteers, especially around fund-raising time.
- Museums and zoos often take on volunteers who act as guides.
- Outreach programs like Meals on Wheels use lots of volunteers.
- Many politicians use volunteers to handle constituent services.

If those options seem too mainstream, think about the causes that matter to you:

- If you are pro-choice, consider whether you could deal with being an escort at a family services clinic.
- If you are concerned about the environment, check out the recycling center.

- Scan the bulletin board at the nearest food co-op to see if there's a group putting on an event like an Earth Day celebration.
- Your local public interest research group (PIRG) may need help. Volunteers there often do grunt work on social justice issues like redlining.
- Many states have a state office to help promote local volunteer work, or a private organization that serves a similar function. Here are a few of them:

Alabama
Governor's Office of Community and National Service
600 Dexter Avenue
Montgomery, AL 36130
(334) 242-7100

Arkansas
Arkansas Office of Volunteerism
P.O. Box 1437
Little Rock, AR 72203
(501) 682-7540

Connecticut
Governor's Council on Voluntary Action
c/o Planning & Management Office
80 Washington Street
Hartford, CT 06106
(203) 566-8320

Delaware
Division of Volunteerism
P.O. Box 637
Dover, DE 19903-0637
(302) 739-4456

Hawaii
Statewide Volunteer Service
Office of the Governor
State Capitol
Honolulu, HI 96813
(808) 586-7200

Illinois
Illinois Commission on Community Service
100 West Randolph, 3rd Floor
Chicago, IL 60601
(312) 814-5225

Indiana
Governor's Voluntary Action Program
1 North Capitol
Indianapolis, IN 46294
(317) 232-2504

Iowa
Office of the Governor
State Capitol
Des Moines, IA 50319
Att'n: Bobbie Finch
(515) 281-8304

Minnesota
Minnesota Office of Citizenship and Volunteer Services
117 University Avenue
St. Paul, MN 55155
(612) 296-4731

New Hampshire
Governor's Office on Volunteerism
The State House Annex, Room 431
25 Capitol Street
Concord, NH 03301
(603) 271-3771

New Jersey
The Governor's Office on Volunteerism
222 S. Warren Street
CN700
Trenton, NJ 08625
(609) 984-3470

North Carolina
Governor's Office of Citizen Affairs
116 West Jones Street

Raleigh, NC 27603
(919) 733-2391

North Dakota
Office of Volunteer Services
Department of Human Services
Judicial Wing, 3rd Floor
600 East Boulevard Avenue
Bismarck, ND 58505
(701) 328-4808

Oregon
Assistant to the Governor for Special Projects
State Capitol Building, Room 160
Salem, OR 97310
(503) 378-4584

Pennsylvania
Penn-SERVE
Governor's Office of Citizen's Service
Room 1304
Labor & Industry Building
Harrisburg, PA 17120
(717) 787-1971

Rhode Island
Volunteer in Action, Inc.
168 Broad Street
Providence, RI 02903-4028
(401) 421-6547

South Carolina
Volunteer Services Liaison
Office of the Governor
1205 Pendleton Street
Columbia, SC 29201
(803) 734-0398

Tennessee
Administrative Services
Tennessee Dept. of Human Services

How to Make Use of a Useless Degree

400 Deadrich Street
Nashville, TN 37248
(615) 313-4706

Vermont
Director of Public Information
Governor's Action Line
109 State Street
Montpelier, VT 05609
(802) 828-3333

Wyoming
Wyoming Volunteer Assistance Corp.
Box 4008, University Station
Laramie, WY 82071
(307) 766-2477

94 🦉 Advocate

Hannah works in the Public Education Department of a civil rights organization.

"Just because you work for a nonprofit doesn't mean you avoid politics and organizational issues. Those problems are still there. But they are a little easier to tolerate. It does get tiring, after a while, doing everything in a resource-poor environment.

"One drawback to working in an issue-based organization is that people always want to debate you. I don't agree with 100 percent of the stands the organization takes, and it can get awkward sometimes. But, given how reactionary the country's getting, some of us have to stand up and be liberals."

How did you get the job?

"I answered an ad in the paper and didn't get the job. Six months later, they called me. They had said they would keep my resumé on file, and they did. My boyfriend thinks that's the only time in history that's actually happened."

A Few Good Organizations

There are thousands of good causes—and organizations, some good, for all of them. Here are a few:

- American Foundation for AIDS Research (AmFAR)
  733 3rd Avenue - 12th Floor
  New York, NY 10017
  (212) 682-7440
  AmFAR is the primary private funder of research on the treatment and prevention of AIDS.

- The American Red Cross
  430 17th Street, NW
  Washington, DC 20006
  (800) 272-0094
  There when there's an emergency.

- Amigos de las Americas
  5618 Star Lane
  Houston, TX 77057
  (713) 782-5290
  Participants are sent on four- to eight-week programs throughout South America after several months of training and preparation.

- Amnesty International
  322 Eighth Avenue
  New York, NY 10001
  (212) 807-8400
  A favorite cause for rock stars. They speak out for political prisoners around the world, even in the U.S.

- Common Cause
  2030 M Street, NW
  Washington, DC 20036
  (202) 833-1200

Working for open government and a freer flow of information.

- Habitat for Humanity International
121 Habitat Street
Americus, GA 31709
(912) 924-6935
The outfit Jimmy and Rosalynn Carter are associated with. They build homes for low-income people.

- The Hunger Project
15 East 26th Street, #1401
New York, NY 10010
(212) 532-4255
The Hunger Project is a global, strategic organization committed to finding sustainable solutions for hunger, worldwide. In other words, they attack hunger by addressing the root causes that lead to hunger.

- NAACP Legal Defense and Education Fund, Inc.
99 Hudson Street, 16th Floor
New York, NY 10013
(212) 219-1900
Fighting discrimination with litigation in employment, housing, education, and other areas.

- National Coalition for the Homeless
1612 K Street, NW, Suite 1004
Washington, DC 20006
(202) 775-1322
Volunteers staff "transitional homes" and help the homeless to find independent housing.

- Peace Corps
1990 K Street, NW
Washington, DC 20526
(800) 424-8580
One of the great remaining legacies of the Kennedy Administration, the Peace Corps places several thousand volunteers each year, mainly in rural settings in developing countries.

- Planned Parenthood
  Check your local phone book for the office near you. They do more than provide birth control and family planning services; they also help new parents.

- Volunteers for Peace
  43 Tiffany Road
  Belmont, VT 05730
  (802) 259-2759
  Places multinational teams of volunteers in thirty-six countries, on social, environmental, conservation, restoration, archeological, and agricultural projects.

- WorldTeach
  Harvard Institute for International Development
  1 Eliot Street
  Cambridge, MA 02138
  (617) 495-5527
  This program places college graduates as teachers in foreign countries. An up-front fee to cover training and placement is required. Knowledge of teaching English as a second language is preferred, though some participants teach subjects other than English.

- Young Men's Christian Association (YMCA)
  Check your local phone book, or contact the national office at
  101 North Wacker Drive
  Chicago, IL 60606
  (312) 280-3400
  Providers of a wide range of community services, and often a good place to stay for a while or find a reasonably priced gym.

- Young Women's Christian Association (YWCA)
  Check your local phone book, or contact the national office at
  726 Broadway
  New York, NY 10003
  (212) 614-2700

Like the YMCA, providers of a wide range of community services, and often a good place to stay for a while or find a reasonably priced gym.

95 🦉 Environmental Activist

Lil works to save the environment.

"The folks at Worldwatch predict that we have only twenty years to reverse the industrial, environmental degradation of the earth. After that, it's an unstoppable downward spiral. Given that, how can you justify doing anything other than working for the environment?

"Future generations are going to judge our generation poorly, but the people who put themselves on the line to protect the environment will be heroes. We're the ones with vision; we're the ones who care about the future. What courage is there in cutting down a redwood or setting off a nuclear test or harpooning a whale? Absolutely none. But getting between the tree and the saw, the boat and the blast site, or the harpoon and the whale—that's courage, that's commitment, and it's the only logical choice for a caring, thinking person.

"Forget saving for your future and your kids' future. There will be no future if we don't reverse things now."

How did you get the job?

"I volunteered."

A Few Green Organizations

- Audubon Society
  700 Broadway
  New York, NY 10003
  (212) 979-3000

One of the most venerable environmental institutions, which in recent years has developed a stance "more activist" than its old image.

- Center for Marine Conservation
  1725 DeSales Street, NW, Suite 500
  Washington, DC 20036
  (202) 429-5609
  Best friends to seals, otters, and many more.

- Environmental Defense Fund
  257 Park Avenue South
  New York, NY 10010
  (212) 505-2100
  Public campaigns about recycling and other important issues.

- Greenpeace USA
  1436 U Street, NW
  Washington, DC 20009
  (202) 462-1177
  One of the most outspoken and "activist" groups.

- National Geographic Society
  1145 17th Street
  Washington, DC 20036
  (202) 857-7000
  They do more than make pretty magazines. Call them and find out.

- National Wildlife Federation
  1400 Sixteenth Street, NW
  Washington, DC 20036-2266
  (202) 797-6800
  A voice for the endangered species.

- Natural Resources Defense Council
  40 West 20th Street
  New York, NY 10011
  (212) 727-2700
  Focused on raising public awareness of wasteful or toxic business practices and consumer products.

- The Nature Conservancy
  1815 North Lynn
  Arlington, VA 22209
  (703) 841-5300
  Works to protect sensitive habitat by purchasing it.

- The Sierra Club Foundation
  730 Polk Street
  San Francisco, CA 94109-7813
  (415) 776-2211
  One of the older and more respected environmental organizations.

- United States Environmental Protection Agency (EPA)
  401 M Street, SW
  Washington, DC 20460
  (202) 262-5055
  Regulating air and water quality, with a focus on restricting or cleaning up toxic chemicals.

- United States Forest Service, Regional Office
  Pacific-Northwest Region
  P.O. Box 3623
  Portland, OR 97208-3623
  (503) 326-3651
  Volunteer opportunities in wildlife management, campground maintenance, and conservation projects in Montana, Idaho, and the Dakotas.

- United States Forest Service, Regional Office
  Pacific Northwest Region
  P.O. Box 3623
  Portland, OR 97208-3623
  Opportunities for volunteer work in the nineteen national forests of Oregon and Washington.

- Wilderness Society
  900 17th Street NW
  Washington, DC 20006
  (202) 833-2300

Focused on public lands policy, most specifically on policies and practices affecting National Wilderness Areas, parklands, and national forests.

- World Wildlife Fund/The Conservation Foundation
1250 24th Street, NW, Suite 500
Washington, DC 20037
(202) 293-4800
Protecting nature from humans. Working to preserve endangered species around the world.

LEARN A TRADE

One way to solve the job dilemma is to learn a trade. It may mean going to a trade school, or apprenticing yourself for a while. And you'll have to resolve yourself to the fact that you've ended up doing something that you didn't have to go to college to do. (That shouldn't be hard to do—you still benefited from college, and you probably didn't go to college just to get a job.)

These five people have learned a trade, and have marketable expertise.

96 🦉 Masseuse

Fiona is a masseuse.

"OK, let's get it out in the open: I'm not a prostitute. I really am a masseuse. A licensed massage therapist, if you will. You can submit my services to your health plan, if they are prescribed, and sometimes they'll pay. My table cost more than you can imagine. This is legitimate, and the best thing you can do for yourself.

"I work at a health club and at home, by appointment only. You, for example, are carrying a lot of tension in your shoulders. If you never get that released, it will cripple you by the time you're old. I do Swedish massage, but I've studied shiatsu and rolfing, too.

"The strangest thing that happens is that people fall asleep by the end of a massage. The room is so relaxing, and they've released so much tension that they drift off. If I don't have anyone right after them, I let them sleep."

Best source of customers?

"Spouses. If one gets a massage, the other will try one within a month. I'm not sure why."

The Jobless Recovery

It used to be that when the economy improved, more people were hired, and people negotiated for raises. Now, however, we have what's known as "the jobless recovery." Indicators are up, companies are making more money, but they aren't hiring. In fact, many of them are continuing to downsize.

People are being treated the same way inventory is. Instead of building supplies and staffs that they will need, companies are waiting till the last minute and hiring "just in time."

The fact that people still call it a recovery, even though no jobs are recovered, says a lot about where priorities are these days: certainly not with keeping citizens employed.

97 🦉 Bookkeeper

Remi is a bookkeeper.

"Bookkeeping is a great trade. Every organization has to keep records, and there's really only one right way to keep them, with a few important variations. Not everyone has the time or the temperament to keep books, but I do. I'm, as they say, compulsive. I learned accounting in night school: it was easier than any college course I took.

"I keep books for four different companies, one day a week for each. The hard part is starting up with a company. It always takes weeks to straighten up what they've been doing, and weeks to get them accustomed to proper procedures."

Best source of customers?

"A tax lawyer."

Temp Agencies as Employment Agencies

A lot of companies are using temp agencies as employment agencies. They bring people in and have a nice long trial period to see if they like them. Temp firms know this, and have "out" clauses in their contracts which compensate them when temps are turned into employees. And, of course, some companies try to find ways to cheat.

Companies have been known to ask temp employees to tell their temp firm they have moved out of town, or to come back to the company after working somewhere else

How to Make Use of a Useless Degree

for six months and a day, just so the company can get out of paying the temp firm whatever fee they would contractually owe if they hired a temp full time. Many temps feel no loyalty to the temp firms that have been profiting from their hard work and are happy to conspire with the company. But when you can, it's clearly better to stay out of the debate between the temp firm and the company.

98 🦉 Carpenter

Bonzo is a carpenter who travels a lot and builds things that aren't meant to last.

"As the carpenter for the tour of a very physical dance theater production, I have to build stuff that the cast can climb, hang off of, and jump on. But since we move on after a day or two, I have to be able to break it down quickly.

"Theoretically, there should be some formulaic, modular way of doing this, but that's not how it works. Every theater presents a new problem. Spaces are very different. What's hidden in one place is exposed in another. Build it the wrong way for the local fire code, and some marshal will have you tearing it down an hour before the curtain.

"I'd like to claim that I studied a lot to learn how to do all this, but my skills, my tools, and my infinite respect for duct tape have been acquired on the job."

How did you get the job?

"I volunteered at a performance art space, and as the producers became more respectable, they remembered me."

To Tie, or Not to Tie?

There's no question that the tie is one of the most useless pieces of apparel ever created, but in some jobs a guy's going to have to wear one.

At other places—in machine shops, for example—wearing a tie creates a safety hazard. There, steel-toed boots and goggles are more appropriate.

Dressing for work is a lot like dressing for your first week of high school: you don't want to stand out until you have a good sense of how people dress where you're going to be working. Some places have written dress codes. A lot more have unspoken dress codes which are every bit as strict.

One person we interviewed got lectured for showing up at an advertising agency wearing a Brooks Brothers all-cotton oxford button-down dress shirt—the boss disapproved because it was a short-sleeved shirt. The boss man, incidentally, was wearing a cape and carrying a purse.

Watch out for casual Friday! A lot of companies have started to have "Casual Fridays"—days when people are allowed to dress a little more casually than the other days of the week. If you interview on a Friday, be sure to ask how people dress the other days of the week.

And with most salaried jobs, work is not the place to be sexy. (Work is complicated enough without . . .) In some situations, such as waiting on tables, you may get better tips for looking sexy. That's your call. Just be sure that whatever you're wearing, you're ready to wear it for a whole shift, and on the way back home.

Whatever you wear to work, have more than one set of it. Sooner or later you'll have to do the laundry.

99 🦉 Archivist

George is an archivist.

"Companies are just starting to learn how important it is to preserve their histories. It's not just a matter of history and culture, it's also a matter of legality.

"In the past week, I've been researching our first marine insurance policy for a newsletter article, compiling a list of our

How to Make Use of a Useless Degree

firsts for a sales meeting AV, getting some notes together for a retirement party speech on what was happening here forty years ago, and finding all the documentation we have that might pertain to a Superfund case from a client that we had twenty years ago.

"There is really too much here for me to do, and every week I hear of something that's being thrown out from some office somewhere in the country. And since I'm not connected to a revenue stream, I have no idea how solid my job is. But if I'm not here, there are always museums and historical societies."

How did you get the job?

"A consultant told the company to search their history for core corporate culture values. The people in the company thought it was bullshit, so they gave me the job as a summer intern. I wrote a report that they liked so much they edited it into a brochure."

Resumé Inflation

If you have problems putting your accomplishments into this kind of highly favorable perspective, just think of it as advertising. Many of us grew up hearing ads that said that "Wonder Bread helps build strong bodies in twelve ways." I'm sure it does. We also imagine that other breads are even better for you. If Wonder Bread can make such bold claims, so can you.

If you parked cars, you were entrusted with machinery worth tens of thousands of dollars. If you caddied at a golf course, you have proven that you can mix well with executives. If you sold Girl Scout cookies, you have experience selling. If you played a team sport, you know something about teamwork.

Don't go overboard. It won't help your resumé, or your chances, if you say that you ran the Westinghouse Corporation during college summers, or that your first job was being a Supreme Court justice.

100 🦉 Framer

Sylvia is a framer (of art, not of houses).

"I learned framing before college and it's let me make decent money while in college, graduate school, and now. In Oregon, in New York, and in Champaign/Urbana there are framing shops ready to hire any steady, experienced pair of hands. It also helps that I know what archival standards are and can talk to customers about rag mats, no-glare glass, and all that.

"There are mechanics to this, but also a sensibility. I have an eye for what's right, and what's not. I have occasionally called customers and asked them to reconsider their specifications. I won't get rich doing this, but even in bad times people at least frame diplomas and awards."

How did you get the job?

"I learned framing in high school when I helped the art teacher mount exhibits. After that, I just looked for frame shops in the Yellow Pages, walked in, and said, 'I can do that.' "

You Don't Have to Be a Leader

A lot of companies say that they are looking to hire leaders, and that's intimidating to people who know, in their heart of hearts, that they just aren't the leader type.

Don't worry. Some companies like to hire people who have been in the military, and they say they're hiring leaders. But in the services, the first thing you learn to do is follow orders. Companies are perfectly willing, and even eager, to hire followers, and just plain individuals, too.

BACK TO SCHOOL

The last thing you can do with your useless degree is, of course, go back to school.

101 🦉 Student

Sasha went back to school. Law school, to be exact.

"I tried to find a job that was satisfying, but I got nowhere. I had rejected the idea of law school because I saw law as excessively property oriented, as argumentative and unnecessary. But after a few years of trying to get things done for environmental causes, I've realized that I could do a lot more as a lawyer.

"With legal training, I'll know more about how to approach corporations with resolutions that their lawyers will let them sign. And a law degree will help enormously with international negotiations. People in other countries tend to treat lawyers with enormous respect.

"I wasn't ready for law school when I got out of college. Now I am."

Apply for Grants

Grants are like scholarships for things after college (often for more school). Most of the really big grants go to organized students with fantastic academic records who were filling out applications and interviewing while you were busy studying the perverse physics of Jell-O shots, but there's no reason why you can't apply for next year and use that as an excuse to spend the intervening months perfecting your backhand.

Go back to your college, if you still live nearby, and meet the career counselor whom you avoided. He or she may have information about all sorts of grants.

The best of all grants is the MacArthur Grant: it's generous, there are no applications, and no restrictions. Unfortunately, these "genius" grants are generally given out on the basis of previous accomplishments, so few recent grads get them.

Still, it's something to dream about.

 # Afterword:

What to do with an (almost) useless paycheck

Just as getting your degree may not have turned out to be the ticket to easy instant success, getting a paycheck may not turn out to be as rich an experience as you expect. For a while, you're likely to be pretty far down on the food chain, in a society that urges you to buy, buy, buy.

Here are some money-related tips we heard from people we interviewed:

Transportation

"Don't even think of buying a new car. Buy used."

"Learn how to change your oil."

"Carpool. Gas costs really add up."

"Bicycle. It's better for the earth, better for you, and a whole lot cheaper."

Food and Drink

"Learn to cook. I ate out every day for a year, and ended up with credit card balances that I'll be paying for years."

"Join a food co-op."

"Drink water. I know it sounds silly, but I save a couple of bucks a day by drinking water instead of soda."

"Buy store-brand foods."

"Buy beans and rice in bulk and live on them. You can't afford meat, in any sense of the word."

"Learn to love leftovers. Tabasco sauce helps."

Entertainment

"The library. Mine has CDs as well as books."

"Wait for the video. Most movies aren't worth what theaters charge."

"Offer to usher at theaters. That way you get in free."

"Make tapes of friends' CDs."

Housing

"Don't live in a good school district if you don't have kids. Housing costs more there."

"Roommates—I could never cover the rent on my own."

"Use ads and bulletin boards, not brokers."

Communications

"Wait for your parents to call you."

"Communicate on-line; it's cheaper than the phone."

"Ask for people's Fed Ex numbers, so you can send 'collect' packages."

"Know when you can make cheaper phone calls."

Travel

"Fly stand-by."

"If you have executive parents like mine, ask if you can use their frequent flyer points."

"House swap with friends."

Recycle

"Get your clothes from Goodwill."

"Cycle your presents. Give away stuff you got to someone you want to give something to."

"Erase and reuse the computer disks that on-line services send you."

Extra Income

"Pick up pennies when you see them."

"Collect and return deposit cans. I collect them from the lanes and parking lots where high school kids go drinking."

"Sell those old textbooks. Realistically, you'll never reread them."

"Get a second job."

Mooch

"Go home to do your laundry."

"Eat all you can at parties."

"Use the office mailroom. The executives do it."

General

"Offer to pay in cash if the seller will give you a discount."

"File expense reports for everything. There's no reason for you to subsidize the company."

"Submit all medical expenses. That's what insurance is for."

"Take every tax deduction you can."

"Skip the Thanksgiving pilgrimage home."

"Never pay full price. Shop for sales."

"Beware of credit cards. They're worse than drugs."

"Save. It sounds old-fashioned, but it's important."

WITHDRAWN

p. p. 220